Co-Bully
NO MORE

Co-Bully
NO MORE

Copyright © 2017 by Judith Carmody

Publisher:
Judith Carmody
Email: info@judithcarmody.com

Website: www.judithcarmody.com

Twitter.com/judithcarmody1

Facebook.com/authorjudithcarmody1

Linkedin.com/in/judith-carmody-author

Publishing consultant:
Professional Woman Publishing, LLC
www.pwnbooks.com

ISBN: 978-0-9955931-0-7

Disclaimer:
The views contained in this book are solely to create awareness.
Please consult your Health Care Professionals for personal
advice.

WITH LOVE AND GRATITUDE ...

Mum, My Earth Angel

I am there holding and protecting you,
My love circles you, in everything you do.
Twinkling star I will always shine through,
a promise I am forever with you.

Contents

About the Author   ix
Introduction   1

CHAPTER 1

What is a Healthy Relationship?   3
What is an Abusive Relationship?   5
What is a Self-Relationship?   6
Emotional Health   6
YES to: Your Emotional Smart School   7
Unconditional Love   8
Conditional Love   9
Self-Love   9

CHAPTER 2

Aggressive, Manipulative Communication   11
Emotional Abusers Need A Target   13
Recognise The Covert Trap   13
In Order to Understand People Susceptible to
Emotional Abuse Recognise a Pattern of Behaviour   14
Learn to Love, Care and Protect Yourself   16

CHAPTER 3

Emotional and Spiritual well-being is the core of a healthy, SPECIAL "self"   19
To Know Yourself – Your Sense of Belonging   20
Self-Esteem   23
Where and how do you get Self-Esteem?   24
The Feeling of being Lovable and the Feeling of being Capable   27
Awareness and Support   29

CHAPTER 4

Definition of a Co-Bully   31
Definition of a Bully   32
Co-Dependency   33
Striving Instead of Thriving   34

CHAPTER 5

Characteristics of a Co-Bully   37
Zoning in on Threatening Moods   39
A Bully doesn't come Dressed as a Monster, they are Everyday People   40
Roles Assumed by a Co-Bully   41
Positive Energy – Negative Energy Positive Feelings – Negative Feelings   42
Enabler   44
People Pleaser   45
Rescuer/Fixer   46
The Caretaker   47
Caring and being Cared for   48
Peacemaker   49
Fear of Rejection   49
Powerful Vs Powerless   50

CHAPTER 6

Characteristics of the Bully   51
Taker   53
Rebel   54
A Controller   54
Narcissist   54
Negative Emotions   57
Disconnected from Their True Self   59
Take Control – Seek Professional Help   60

CHAPTER 7

Emotional Abuse   61
Discipline   66
Formation of the Emotional Abuser's Personality   67
Begin to Assert Separateness from the Controller   67

CHAPTER 8

Signs of an Emotionally Abusive Relationship	72
Forgiveness is for the Person Abused, Not the Abuser	72
Self-Forgiveness	74

CHAPTER 9

Related Personality Disorders	79
Negative Behaviour	79

CHAPTER 10

Recovery after Abuse	85
Personal Boundaries	88

CHAPTER 11

Healing – Self Compassion	89
Empathy	92
Let go and Let God	95
Understanding what Letting Go is	96
Self Awareness	98
Break Free from Co-Dependency	101
Codependent Behaviors	103
Treating Codependency	105

CHAPTER 12

Conscious and Unconsciousness	109
True Self and Shadow/Ego	111
Control	115
God's Consciousness	116

CHAPTER 13

Emotional Awareness	119
Listening Skills	123
Communication Skills	123
Moving Forward with Skills to Manage Your Emotional Safety	123
Self-Love V Materiality Love	125
Meditation	126
Thoughts	127
References	137

About the Author

Name: Judith Carmody

Email: *info@co-bully.com*

Website: *www.co-bully.com*

Judith is a CPA, (Certified Public Accountant), with a Masters Degree in Finance. She is a published Author and Poet. She completed a foundation in counselling and a research thesis in communication. She uses her experiences in the Irish school system, the private sector, public sector, corporate workplaces and industries in Ireland, Boston, New York and London to explore social, communication and human resource systems. Her background in management includes the overview of key financial systems. The implementation of process and methodologies in relation to financial planning, service planning, personnel management and per-formance. She developed business cases to support these strategic plans. She is a member of the Munster Certified Public Accountant Society and was a Joint Treasurer from 2006 to 2012. A member of the National Administration Committee for National Strategy 2003 to 2012. Completed Train the Trainer in 2008.

Judith is from Co Kerry, Ireland where the landscape greets the Atlantic Ocean in its Divinity. It gives her spirit and light to write.

Book:	Co-Bully No More
Co-Author:	Finding Your Voice. The Assertive & Empowered Woman
Poetry:	Mirror of Light

Judith has over thirty years' experience working in diverse and in multi-cultural environments. This has given her a great insight into assertive and non-assertive, healthy and unhealthy environments. She introduces awareness and skills to survive and thrive in both. She also creates the awareness that there is support and information available to develop skills to self-manage in challenging relationships. She introduces the term co-bully so people can identify, create awareness of their passive role in relationships, of co-dependency and through the POWER OF CHOICE develop skills to change this pattern. It also creates awareness of communicators who negatively impact on others. They too can develop skills and choose "not to diminish people" in their relationships. This will open up a clear understanding and a separate path to embrace and begin their journey to safely cherish self-empowerment and self-awareness. Awareness comes before personal change. Through self-expression begin a new journey with freedom to self-create and flourish.

Introduction

The aim of this book is to introduce the term "co-bully," and to give a voice, skills and support to those who are experiencing or have experienced bullying behavior.

I want to define the "role" of a co-bully(s) and explain why they may have a high tolerance of inappropriate behavior. This book will create an awareness of "self" and the importance of personal development. It promotes the importance of vocabulary skills to express personal safety and boundaries.

It also encourages the co-bully to develop the ability to articulate and "stop" tolerating relationship abuse as the "norm". This book examines relationship dynamics and explains what actually happens to a "target" during an episode(s) of bullying behavior. This book asks the reader to question their own communication patterns, whether assertive, direct, indirect, or aggressive.

Co-Bully No More, provides insights into how you can break free from a pattern of control, manipulation entanglement and surviving in fear.

I hope this book will enable people who are trapped and hurting today, to see that they have a choice "to be" and to remove themselves from debilitating and dangerous relationships.

It may also help a bully to understand how their inappropriate behaviour adversely affects another person's well-being. They may also self-examine and seek to change their role in a relationship.

This book highlights the human side of emotional abuse and the suffering attached. Co-bullies self-blame when a relationship fails, and this contributes towards their feeling of failure in a relationship. It is also why they stay too long in harmful situations to the detriment of their own well-being. They believe the bully will change or he/she will take responsibility in some way when the relationship breaks down.

This book gives a clear message to the co-bully, that only they can change their passive role. They need to be clearly AWARE WHEN THERE IS A DANGER OR THREAT TO THEIR WELL -BEING and self-protect rather than trying to appease the aggressor or manipulator.

How you act, interact and react with people determines whether you flourish with supportive healthy people or struggle to survive in relationships that are unsafe, unloving, unsupportive, controlling, neglectful or abusive. A safe relationship is love, care and protection and any relationship that is unsafe and full of fear should not be tolerated. I want to share my journey with you so that you know you are not alone, and that there are others who have been in your place.

With self-awareness, you will gain the tools to confront, self-care or exit hurtful relationships. Bullies make you feel alone, lacking and unloved. I hope you learn that you are not alone.

This book will give you the understanding to process your conditioned role and to know that YES you can change that role. I hope to reignite trust and for you to know you are enough. You deserve a life where you are at ease and have safe and loving relationships. You can choose to live a life of love without fear.

CHAPTER 1

*"No problem can be solved from the same level
of consciousness that created it."*

–Albert Einstein

What is a Healthy Relationship?

From the moment of birth you are forming relationships: a self-relationship, close relationships and relationships with "others". Your close relationships are with mothers, fathers, prime care givers, siblings, extended family, and other relationships with community, cultural or society. Your family of origin's pattern of communication which usually consists of parents and prime caregivers, will have a major impact on how you learn to communicate. You develop methods of interacting, surviving, and coping in an adult world. By the time you are three or four years old, school, culture and society will have influenced how you communicate. Schools and culture have a major impact on how we learn to communicate, through teachers and the school's pervading culture. Ways of communicating: assertive, passive, aggressive or indirect. How you act, interact and react with people, determines whether you flourish with supportive healthy people or struggle to survive in relationships that are unsafe, unsupportive, neglectful or abusive. You unconsciously impart to people how to treat you.

It is the awareness that a healthy, positive relationship is a two-way communication where both parties contribute to love and growth. It is an investment of a person's love, trust and time. If one of the parties is abusive or neglectful of the other's needs, this person is tainting the relationship, which will be dysfunctional, striving on a daily basis, instead of thriving and having the space and support to fulfill one's potential.

- The most important feeling is that you can just "be" yourself (self-awareness), you feel supported or, if you feel threatened, neglected or mistreated, you can exit the relationship safely.

- The most important factor is assertive communication. You feel safe to voice your opinions and have skills to self-manage in the presence of anger or neglect. It is important to have self-expression. Communication is supportive, honest and loving. Communication should not involve manipulation, diminishment, threats or put downs.

- Relationships are respectful, flexible and meet the needs of both participants.

- Healthy relationships are between people who are self-aware and do not rely on other peoples' opinions, and who are not approval dependent.

- Healthy communicators do not criticize or judge other people

- A person feels supported, safe, and enjoys the company.

- A person does not feel stressed or frightened.

- A person isn't made feel inadequate or lacking.

- A person is in a place where they can grow to their true potential with support.

What is an Abusive Relationship?

An abusive relationship is wherein one person(s) is a perpetrator of emotional abuse, either covertly or overtly who manipulates, dominates and controls another person(s) for their own benefit and demands. The perpetrator may be controlling, neglectful or dismissive of the other person's needs. There is a dominant person in the relationship thereby the other person becomes the receptive, passive or submissive person. One person may manipulate the trust and honesty of the other person and inflict unsuspecting betrayal. Betrayal is a weapon that causes immense pain and suffering when an intimate bond has been violated or discarded. Trust makes you grow with a person and when you believe in the person and in the relationship, you allow them into your world and feel you can be as one with them. When a person believes they are in a trustful and safe relationship, this unspoken trust is an ultimate bond of any friendship or healthy relationship. When that bond is betrayed without any concern for the deceived person, it is a deep emotionally felt deception. A breach of trust is abuse. This leaves the abused traumatised and left as if part of them is lost or violated. It desecrates their core being and their feeling of safety.

An abuser uses threats, anger, intimidation, and manipulation to diminish and keep the other person under their control. They use tactics to make you feel over-powered, or they create an atmosphere of conflict, confusion and chaos.

- If you feel uneasy, fearful and stressed, you are in an abusive relationship.
- If you feel threatened and the abuser uses put downs, these are signs of dominance and control.
- If you haven't the freedom to "be" or the support or encouragement to grow, you are being manipulated.

What is a Self-Relationship?

The most important relationship on this earth is the relationship we have with ourselves. If we have a loving self-relationship it will extend to all relationships with others and with the universe. It is an awareness of how you see, feel and love yourself. Our true-self is our connection to our core that feels alive and is filled with love and abundance. The most devastating feeling for a person is a sense of "no-self" or self-hate. Unfortunately, a child who was not nurtured and loved will survive in fear and will develop a false or co-dependent self or "ego," and will live a life struggling to survive. He/she will experience and get caught up in difficult relationships with unresolved emotional trauma. It is so important to nourish a good self-relationship from early childhood because it is the only guaranteed relationship you will have in this life. It is important to become consciously aware of your "self" and connect to your higher consciousness. A neglected, abandoned self will lead to the development of a co-dependent self, a disconnected self which forms a pattern of entanglement in neglectful and abusive relationships. Personal power is relationship power. A healthy "self" recognizes when a communicator or a relationship is unhealthy and is able to self-manage or exit. A healthy "self" will not tolerate or permit an unhealthy communicator to diminish or create fear or harm to their self-value or their self-love.

Emotional Health

To question and understand how you act, interact and react in relationships, you will need to understand your emotional health. Emotional health is your well-being, how you feel about yourself, if you feel well or if you feel uneasy, stressed or distressed in a relationship. Emotional health stems from having had a loving and a supportive childhood. It is the emotional health of the communicator that is the determining factor as to whether a relationship is healthy or not. No matter how a person tries to conceal their inner mental-emotional state, it will eventually surface; it is what is sensed, felt and how a person will interact and react to another person. **The emotional presence of a person depends on self-awareness.** It is the disconnection from "self" or the unconscious connection to negative emotions or energy that forms a pattern of entanglement or co-dependency. Are you a healthy communicator, or have you adopted passive communication, or learnt to communicate aggressively? Do you communicate through love or fear? Are you dependent on another person's opinion or approval to know yourself or feel good about yourself? Are you independent, dependent or co-dependent? Have you an awareness of self-expression?

YES to: Your Emotional Smart School

The two primary emotions in life are love and fear; if everyone responded to situations through love, the world would be a happier and a more peaceful place. But unfortunately, from a very young age, some people are instilled with fear and it even gets passed down through generations until a person awakens and becomes self-aware. In 2015, a Church representative condoned smacking to discipline children, which begs the question: has society learnt anything from its past? Conditional love instills fear in children and is the basis and beginning of negative and controlling behaviours. Society must create awareness of unconditional love and how to live life through love. With fear grows anger, hatred, jealousy, as well as manipulative, negative, controlling and destructive behaviour. With love there is support, peace, respect, loving behaviour and joy.

When a child is told that they are bold or bad, this instills a deep rooted message in their psyche that there is something wrong with them, that they are not acceptable or lovable, and this in turn instills fear. They unconsciously fear or are afraid in their interaction with other people but especially in close relationships. They become insecure. They carry this fear and it disconnects them from their true self. A child that is caught up in the crossfire of adult's abusive behavior, will be afraid to love. It may be the abusive behaviour towards the child him/herself or the abusive behaviour to other children or adults in their presence. E.g. a parent diminishing the other parent in the child's presence instills fear of the parent in the child, instead of love. They may be afraid to love the passive parent because the aggressive parent has instilled in them that there is something wrong with the passive parent. They may be afraid to love the aggressive parent because there are conditions to be met, so they begin their pattern of conditional love. Now the child is living in a **place of fear to love** and not only becomes disconnected from their core, but from their inner-love and also to outer-love and Divine love.

Unconditional Love

The "emerging self" in childhood must have a safe environment with unconditional love and not rely on the "unhealthy" opinions of others to give them their sense of "self", and a connection to "self". Unconditional love gives security, acceptance, dignity and love. It is essential for the healthy development of a child's sense of self to emerge as a healthy, separate and authentic self. Unconditional love is the total love and forgiveness of one's "self". *You have done the best so far in this life with the support and skills you have been given. You can interact without seeking acceptance or approval from another person. You are not co-dependent, you are separate, and you are love.*

The natural state for the spirit is unconditional love. The natural free flowing giving and receiving of love, care and protection in any relationship, is Divine. Our soul is in harmony with our body, heart and mind. It is the connection to your true self, which is the connection to Higher Love.

Conditional Love

The "emerging self" learns at a very young age that their "worth" or "value" relies on the approval or acceptance of others firstly in the home, then school and society. You have to be good to be loved and included, or you may have been manipulated to meet the demands of a demanding adult to feel accepted. Love and inclusion was a reward for approval or acceptance. Conditional love is the approval of meeting other people's standards. It is the approval of religious, cultural and societies rules of acceptance and inclusion. Otherwise a person may be ostracized or abandoned, and the **weapon used is the withdrawal or rejection of love and inclusion.** This may continue into adulthood. Love or acceptance especially in close relationships has to be earned and conditions have to be met. In a child's world, the only "self" that is loved and accepted is the compliant child that molds into what they perceive is an accepted or loved child.

Self-Love

If you have arrived at this stage of life and have little understanding of self-love, you probably have no awareness of self "love," and up to now didn't give yourself enough love. You probably were hard on yourself, and allowed other people to be hard on you too. You never forgave yourself for things that didn't turn out the way you expected them to turn out. Self-love and self-forgiveness go hand in hand. We were all children once who looked to our prime care givers for love, support, security and dignity (and our prime caregivers were all children once who looked to their prime care givers for love). It is now recognised to date, the world has made a poor effort to give this to children who grow up to be insecure and disconnected, lost adults. Our world history is one of war, violence, torture, betrayal, domination and belittling of our core "self"(s). People who were in responsible positions, had people who looked to them for guidance but instead instilled them with fear and neglect. This has left many people with a sense of no-self, who are left struggling in a world that has an outward approval dependency epidemic with little awareness of self-expression.

The love of our core-self is getting lost. We must take a moment and look at where we have arrived, as some people are more emotionally damaged than others. We can all start our road to recovery to self-awareness, self-love and self-healing. We must be grateful that we have arrived this far under such a threatening environment. We must self-forgive if we have been conditioned *not* to self-love. We were told not to be vain, stop concentrating on ourselves. Self-love is very different than vanity. Self-love is an inner, peaceful love. We all have arrived at where we are with the life skills that were given to us. If we are unhappy, we can embrace new thoughts, life skills, change, and welcome a life of love and gratefulness. We must learn to heal the link between our emotional pain to our thoughts, and replace them with new self-enlightening and loving thoughts. We must have self-appreciation and self-compassion that we have done the best we could so far and value ourselves with love. Life is full of threats and injustices, but we have arrived where we are and that must be appreciated. Society has placed more importance on wealth achievement rather than personal fulfillment of self-love and supreme love. Since childhood, we are addicted to a need to belong; we want to belong to family, friends, society or institutions. If we had self-awareness, then the true "be" longing is to belong and to behold "self". We are running out of ourselves to be fulfilled with conditional love, and materiality, and we are unaware that we have unconditional inner-love in abundance. Self-love and self-forgiveness is the stepping stone to a path whereby you can flourish in harmony with the universe.

CHAPTER 2

*By maintaining personal boundaries, we discourage abuse
and assert our separateness. Hurt, once experienced,
needs to be healed. It will not go away on its own.*

Aggressive, Manipulative Communication

Bullies communicate through control, intimidation, aggression, deception and manipulation. Bullies don't come dressed as monsters; they generally don't look different or act differently on the surface. They are your everyday males, females, young, old, husbands, wives, mothers, fathers, sisters, brothers, managers, colleagues, rich and poor, tall and small. Bullies exist in everyday circles, families, "friends", school or work colleagues. Bullies may appear "normal" until an emotional issue arises, then the tendency towards abuse emerges. Bullies usually bully someone close to them, whether at home, work or school. It is because of this close relationship that the "covert aggressive trap" can take place. A bully will covertly instill fear. If a stranger did what a bully did in an open street, you would be aware of the aggression, and be aware that this person has a dangerous abusive personality disorder. So why is abuse or manipulation more acceptable or more tolerated in a personal relationship, colleague relationship or behind closed doors? Because it is difficult to separate yourself and self-manage when you have built a relationship, invested yourself and your time in it. It might take a week, or a year, or even ten years, but their abusive nature will surface. Unfortunately we don't have an inbuilt alarm system to let us know who is abusive. Bullies are devious and usually "catch" a person unaware or when they are in a vulnerable position. It is why co-bullies self-blame, as they are unaware that they have been targeted by the bully while the bully may still be "acting" nice to other people. Unaware to the co-bully, they are now a "target" that will supply a place for the bully to project their anger or where they can control and manipulate without question.

All bullies have one thing in common, they project their anger, they manipulate, isolate, use put downs, let downs, and always look outwards at the other person to control them and have their needs met. Bullies will usually discard people abruptly and without warning when they cease to find use for that person.

When your "self" has been so damaged by abusers, you have been deeply hurt and made to feel you don't belong, that you are worthless, and you are weak. You believe the injustice is your fault. You look to others for help but may feel worse and more isolated, or you are made feel blame and guilt. If you are trapped in a role of pleasing but only getting abuse, then you must awaken and start living your "life". You must stop being trapped in the role of the "target". You must begin to live your life in abundance, peace and joy. Persistent abusers are selective in who they mistreat. Abuse targets are typically someone close, with whom they have built up a sense of trust. The co-bully is loyal and trustworthy, lacking the skill to retaliate, or is unwilling to report the abuse. Co-bullies can confront the bully, but would never have the express skills to handle the abuse, which will be ongoing if the co-bully gets entangled in it. It is how the bully communicates. Emotional abusive behaviours are typically kept behind closed doors and restricted to moments when there are no witnesses. A person who mistreats you may mistreat only you and may be an acting 'model' citizen to everybody else. Or when you open up and talk about it, you discover that everybody else knew they were abusive but did nothing, as you were the target of abuse, not them. If you are the target of abuse it can be the most hurtful, isolating place in the world. It knocks your confidence, your self-belief and crushes your world. It is also confusing, as they could be "acting" nice to your circle of friends, which they manipulate to make you feel even worse.

Emotional Abusers Need A Target

A bully keeps changing the goalposts, nice when they are getting what they want or explosively angry when they want something or are jealous of someone or something. This is how the bully manipulates, constantly switching between hot and cold. The relationship could be OK for a period, if the bully is happy, but the co-bully is always aware that one day the bully may explode. The target will often comply, grateful for a period of calm, thinking "hopefully they have changed" and hoping not to provoke or cause any further outbursts.

Recognise The Covert Trap

I want to introduce the term 'co-bully' (receptor of emotional abuse), create awareness of the co-bully's conditioned pattern of behavior and offer an explanation of co-dependency to relational emotional abuse. I want to change receptive communication patterns to assertiveness, empowerment, self-awareness to seek healthy support, and change their role to safely act, react and interact with perpetrators of direct (aggressive) and indirect (manipulative) emotional abuse. This book operates on the thesis that the emotionally abused person must recognise that they themselves may only take responsibility for and seek to change their own receptive behaviours, rather than react to the abusive behaviour of another. It also asks to reflect and examine patterns of abuse or mistreatment in the context of their childhood environment.

If the abused refused to assume their expected role, there can be no abuse. Learn to be aware that you are being targeted at the earliest stage possible. The most effective way of stopping abuse is for the co-bully to have awareness of self-love, self-worth, self-protection and the **knowledge that they do not have to permit an aggressor to target them.** You can exit from this situation. Learn to self-manage in the company of bullies, as you will not change their behavior, but you can change your own over time through self-awareness, emotional detachment, language skills and learning assertive communication skills. The only thing you can change is the amount of abuse you take, which should be none. It is as easy as learning the skills to trust your instincts, create the observer "self", detach and remember that you did nothing wrong; bullies make you feel mad or bad (because it entraps you). The most important thing to know is that their abusive behaviour has nothing to do with you, as it is their own mismanaged anger, so remove yourself as quickly as possible before they rope you in and entrap you. Stop placating them, as nothing will change a bully and you, the target, will certainly not change their behaviour. This abusive behaviour towards you will continue as long as you put up with it. **STOP BEING AVAILABLE and stop getting involved with them.** Bullies require professional help to make them aware of their negative, abusive behavior before they can even think about changing it.

In Order to Understand People Susceptible to Emotional Abuse Recognise a Pattern of Behaviour

An emotionally abused child will struggle to understand the behaviour of their adult primary care providers when they impose hurtful, diminishing, abusive methods of interaction under the umbrella of "care". A child will try to pacify and please so they won't be abandoned or rejected. This struggle will continue into adulthood, unable to confront an abuser and will persist in trying to keep the status quo and peace, which will often have a detrimental effect on their own welfare. They will self-neglect in the onslaught of an attack, conflict or abuse, and will self-harm and self-blame. One of the biggest fears for a co-bully is conflict, as this leaves them completely powerless.

The bully will make the co-bully feel it is their fault, who then will try to rescue and adjust the atmosphere at all costs. The co-bully is constantly aware of the atmosphere the bully projects and usually is hyper-vigilant. Bullies initially charm or act nice but can change at the toss of a coin and make a co-bully feel rejection, or projects a threat of punishment which is one of the worst feelings to them. In order to survive, the co-bully tries to create a positive atmosphere, unaware that it is impossible to change the bully. The co-bully tries everything possible to rectify the situation, feeling the humiliation and degradation the bully is inflicting. All the while they are experiencing the confusion of the bully's tactics of playing hot-cold, good-bad, without any warning or explanation. The co-bully is entrapped in this toxic atmosphere, without having rectified support and will continuously try to appease the bully. The co-bully should be aware of the atmosphere the bully is projecting and remove themselves. The co-bully should project their personal safe boundary and assert their separateness. The bully may be extra friendly to the other people in their company to make the co-bully now feel more desperate. The co-bully needs to develop tools quickly to be able to say that the bully's behaviour is dysfunctional and abusive – the co-bully shouldn't zone in on them emotionally, as it is debilitating and exhausting. The co-bully could spend years in this thankless repetitive abusive cycle, replacing one bully with the next. The first step is to recognise this projected negative behaviour, the co-bully should say that the bully's abusive behaviour is nothing to do with me, and this is a big step forward. The first step to self-empowerment is to say, **I did nothing wrong, and don't absorb their negative energy or don't let them dump their anger on you** (therefore the bully won't be able to project feelings of guilt or shame). **Say it out loud and believe it.** This is the beginning of putting a protective shield around yourself, putting your well-being first, being assertive and self-protecting probably for the first time.

Learn to Love, Care and Protect Yourself

The reason why some people seem to go with the flow of life while others continually struggle in relationships is simply the fact that the happiest, safest people have self-awareness, love, care and the ability to self-protect and have awareness of self-expression. Their self-value, their emotional core, hasn't been damaged or shattered to the extent that it leads to accepting unhealthy communicative patterns as normal. They act, react and interact healthily, without projecting or absorbing fear. These people, *unlike* the co-bully, can self-manage and are aware from the onset of the bully's destructive emotional behavior, and they will *not permit it or absorb it.* These people are focused on developing their own lives to the best of their ability and have the skills to confront or avoid bullies. These people have supportive networks and have high self-value instilled in them as children and carry it into adulthood. They have the life skills to self-manage around a bully's unwanted behaviour. These people choose healthy supportive relationships. Some people have been conditioned to look outward for approval, unaware that if you look inward you can think highly of yourself irrespective of other peoples' opinions.

Turn the other cheek when a person hurts you, love thy neighbour as thyself (even though they may have tried to kill you!), forgive everyone. Children should be seen and not heard, don't shame the family. Empty vessels make the most sound. I believe the co-bully is conditioned to think of the other person first and molds him/herself to please and pacify the other. It is instilled in their psyche that the other person's feelings are more important than their own.

It would be great to go through life with life skills so you can engage well with family, friends, and work colleagues, without being hurt or putting yourself in diminishing, psychologically dangerous relationships. You recognise an abusive situation and one that is not in your best interest. You have the knowledge and tools to exit an abusive situation in the early stages, without letting the abuse go on for too long. You have the verbal skills to openly express your feelings and not accept the abusive put downs or rants of a bully. You are aware when they try to manipulate you or deceive you. You don't feel you are responsible for anybody else's feeling or anybody else's moods. It is nothing to do with you, and you recognise other people dumping their anger, bitterness, jealousy, and you have the skills not to absorb it, or waste your time, health and energy trying to resolve it. Trying to calm them and make them happy. **IT IS NOT YOUR DUTY.**

Unfortunately, some people communicate through argument; it could be your family, workplace, or circle of friends, and no matter how you try to fix or pacify them, it is impossible. You will be constantly drawn into conflict, hostility and a soul destroying way of living. You must detach yourself, and surround yourself with peaceful, like-minded people, who want to live their life through peace and joy. A co-bully must stop taking another's abusive behaviour personally and know it is the bully's own mismanaged anger. They must recognise abuse at the onset and detach.

The only duty you have on this earth is the duty to yourself, to have a loving self-relationship, to care for your "self" and to protect your "self". When you self-love and self-care you will only choose healthy relationships and focus on creating your dreams. You will be on your physical journey to become a Higher Soul. The bully isn't wasting their time by being upset or wondering if they hurt your feelings. Unfortunately, the co-bully has learnt along the way that if a person insults them, they absorb the negative energies rather than having a boundary. Learn not to absorb it and know their behaviour is nothing to do with you.

A co-bully has a compulsive need for approval even when the bully is blatantly abusing them. It is leaving your "core" unattended and looking outwards to feel whole. If you could look "inwards", everything you need is there; self-approval, self-love, self-care, self-protection, self-expression, consciousness, and your connection to Higher Love. **You can be safe in your own place, your connection to self-belonging, a sense of self-beauty in the light of Divine Beauty.**

To embrace true self-love we must be our own best friend, not judge or condemn ourselves and not permit another person to judge or condemn us, as nobody has a right to do that. To have a true self-relationship is to self-love. Our core spirit is self-love which is all healing, growth and har-mony. Ego thrives on power, control, jealousy and survival of the fittest, with no empathy or understanding for others or their survival. There will be no support when needed.

CHAPTER 3

Our Educational and Social Systems have conditioned
us to become fragmented as a human "being",
we must find our path to become
a "whole being" again.

Emotional and Spiritual well-being is the core of a healthy, SPECIAL "self"

A nurtured child evolves and emerges their true self with the love and support of healthy caregivers. This enables a child to develop naturally. A child will connect to their inner feelings of self-love and self-value. The child will be self-connected both emotionally and spiritually. They will have a consciousness of self-expression. The nurtured healthy child will develop self-awareness, have self-value, personal boundaries, the ability to be self-reliant (as per age) and the ability to self-care and self-protect.

To Know Yourself – Your Sense of Belonging

Spiritual Self-Awareness

Your soul is your unique "self", your core and the consciousness of your expression. Your essence, your energy connected to the source energy that is the SPIRIT. A person is love and forgiveness. To know one's "true self" and be aware that a person can only do their best with the awareness they were given in life. A child is a treasure of love from the Universe and doesn't have to prove its value. In times of distress learn to let go, surrender, and know that there is a Higher Power. Let the creative process fill every point of your life that needs healing. Love is ready to do what you cannot do by yourself. Connect to the deep love within yourself. Some people don't know how to self-love or self-forgive, they are caught up in turmoil and chaos, and miss out on love all their lives, love that would make their life happier and more fulfilled. They seem to self-hate rather than self-love, self-harm rather than self-care. It is a difficult to understand but you are where you are meant to be at this time, this is your path. To see the lesson you are given in life, to see negativity as a teacher and learn from it, not become smothered by it, but learn, change your receptive role and embrace every day. Be grateful every morning, breathe in love, and know karma is real. Self-awareness is awakening and connecting to your "Higher Self".

Social Self

Children need to know that everyone is different, that everyone is unique, with a personal set of abilities. With a good, loving, dependable support system one can develop and find much pleasure in life, yet still appreciate, welcome and embrace everyone else's differences and individuality. Human beings are sociable by nature, so partaking, receiving and giving healthy communication is of paramount importance in fulfilling your potential.

Physical Self

To be comfortable and confident in your physical appearance, to be self-appreciative. To know, love, care for and protect yourself. To be aware you are more than your physical self. Your body is your physical self, it is the only "home" or "place" or "space" which is a holding of all of your "self" in this universe. It is your sense of "be" longing and your longing to "be". A person must embrace their place of belonging and never fully belong to people or things outside of them "self". Where you belong is a place of self-acceptance, peace and safety. It is a place of self-dignity and self-value. You are the rightful holder of this place. It is the place where your body and soul exist together. It is your connection and nobody must be permitted to disconnect, distant, or exclude or diminish you. Your "home" or "place" here on earth is your divine connection to your heart and your soul. Your "self" is a gift to be cared for. You hold the key to your own "home" and you must develop an awareness of how to respect and love it and to express to others how to respect and love you.

Emotional health

At the very core of every person is love. Self-love is that part of you that embraces feelings of a human being. It is positive feelings that you are a lovable person and an able person. It is that core emotional evaluation of your self-worth. It is the connection to your true-self. A child needs to feel unconditional love, dignity, a sense of belonging, care and security. A place of love, not fear. Emotional health is self-love and self-forgiveness. Emotional health is having the skills to safely act, react and interact with another human being. **Emotional health affects all aspects of your SPECIAL "self".**

Creative self

When children are in a safe, supportive and protective place, they blossom, flourish and create their life of abundance. They are able to tap into the universe of love and live a life of love not fear. They are supported to take ownership and flow in the rhythm of their self-destiny. The biggest key to creation is gratitude. It is the light of their soul finding a place to "be" visible from an invisible temple. It is the expression of the soul through the "self". Creation unfolds from thoughts, moves to words and is fulfilled in deeds. It manifests into reality. Life becomes "self" creative. You live your life to create your "self" as who you are and who you've always wanted to be for the soul's purpose of evolving.

Intellectual self

To be aware of the world around you, to feel safe and to know there are support systems in place for your well-being. Become self-aware and remove yourself from lower consciousness and become aware of a higher consciousness self. Paint a picture of your "self" of what you wish to project into eternity. You choose what reflects you now and let go of anything that no longer represents you. If you wish to "be" you can embrace new thoughts and accurately reflect whom you now wish to evolve and "be".

Awareness of your mental health

To be aware of your thoughts and beliefs. A lot of thoughts have been inherited or conditioned by primary caregivers, community, religion and culture. If thoughts don't benefit you or support you, or if they are inherited negative ones, **you can change your conditioned belief system** and embrace those to make you feel peaceful, give you a sense of prosperity, wellness and safety. Become consciously aware of your thoughts and behavior patterns. To change is to know and accept you have chosen this previous way of thought but you can change it going forward. Life is a river of changes, go with the flow and choose those which serve your "self" evolving. Change the way you absorb painful experiences and know that pain manifests from wrong thoughts. Develop new thoughts to inspire you to a new understanding. You can free yourself from past fearful thoughts and embrace loving thoughts.

Living, Behavioural self

Is how you behave towards another person and how you permit or allow another person to behave towards you. It is how people interact with each other safely, supportively and lovingly. It is whether a person makes you feel good or feel bad. A person surviving in this world is doing their best. When a person is making their best effort, it should be supported not put down or manipulated. Imposed negativity destroys a person's core ability and infringes their path in life, their positive development, and their confidence. In any relationship, whether short or long, close or distant a person must feel loved and respected.

Self-Esteem

Positive self-esteem is a loving relationship with your "self". It is the feeling of being lovable and the feeling of being capable. *I love who I am.* It is embracing your value and your rightful personal place on this earth. It is a **connection to true expression of your "self"** which connects you to Divine Love. It is the awareness that you have a right to self-love and the right to self-protect. I am enough, I am love. You are SPECIAL, authentic and you have a gift to self-create.

Low self-esteem is a negative evaluation of oneself. It is not liking your "self", it is feeling that you are not good enough, you are worthless, or you are not enough. It is self-hate rather than self-love. It is self-harm rather than self-protection. It is a disconnection from your true "self". It is not having a developed sense of self "value". It is being available to be used and abused. It is not believing or understanding you deserve to be loved in a safe place. It is being co-dependent.

Where and how do you get Self-Esteem?

Psychologist Dr. Tony Humphreys says *children's self-esteem is affected by their prime caregiver's relationships with each other, by the type of loving shown in the family, by the self-esteem of each of the parents, by teachers' interactions with them and by the way that relatives, close family relationships, and all other significant adults interact with each other.*

Cultural, religious, environmental and male/female perceptions in society have an effect on the development of a child's self-esteem. For some children with low self-esteem, home or school may have been a frightening place, with the unpredictability and uncertainty of how they were going to be treated or mistreated on a daily basis with no rights or with little or no support. Being bullied or witnessing bullying has a major negative impact on emotional well-being. When children witness adult's abuse or use other children or adults as a weapon to hurt and to control, this has a lasting effect on their ability to safely interact. Children learn at a very young age to be obedient, not to voice personal opinions and learn very quickly that the "adult" has unquestionable power to oppress, humiliate, intimidate and frighten. The only tool that a child thinks they have is not to further anger either by being obedient, compliant, crying or hoping the abuser will go away.

I now realise as a school child, I was never permitted to freely express myself. I had to think of the consequences if I said something wrong (or right), or something not to the approval of the "adult". I was aware of the punishment and degradation that would be administered with no one to support or no one to say 'stop' and the humiliation imposed from this deranged adult.

When a child has low self-esteem, this will continue into adulthood unless it is recognized, and it can be changed with professional help. If this pattern of behaviour continues into adulthood, it will eventually exhaust and dis-empower the person. A person won't have the energy or hope to continue with this negative pattern of behaviour; therefore they will either have a breakdown or will wake up to "self-awareness" and change. How you feel about yourself will influence every aspect of your life. If you have self-es-teem and have confidence, you will not allow "yourself", your energy or actions to be squandered, wasted or abused. You won't attach or entangle yourself to people or situations which leave you feeling low and worth-less. You will choose friends who have a positive effect on you, guide you, encourage you and, most of all, support and protect you on your journey of life. A person should be aware at an early stage of a relationship if a per-son's behaviour is toxic and you will be able to recognise it and stop it – not absorb it, but instead remove yourself from that abuse. You will know it is not your fault, as their behaviour is nothing to do with you, and you will not be emotionally affected by it or blame yourself for it.

A co-bully can change their presence in a relationship but can never change the toxic behaviour of another. A bully will try to destroy or crush your core self. Life can be very fragile, but with awareness of emotional health, self-esteem, self-love and self-care, you can flourish.

Dr Tony Humphrey's book, **SELF ESTEEM The Key to Your Child's Education**, says *"Your self-esteem forms the centre of your personality and determines the uses you make of your limitless capacity as a human being in your time on earth. It is not your genes which determine your human effectiveness but your self-esteem"*

Bullies are narcissists, controllers, who have a sense of entitlement, have no respect for other people's boundaries, don't care for and don't consider the needs of others. Co-bullies have passive communication skills, supply the demands of others and have no personal safe boundaries.

Patricia said, "Because I was a co-dependent, I had unconsciously surrounded myself with aggressive, manipulators. People that have not been in a similar position will not understand, but will say, why didn't you leave, why did you put up with it?"

The bully and the co-bully are both enacting conditioned behaviour unconsciously. The narcissist has a great way of manipulating people and as for a co-narcissist/co-bully, it is as much their unfortunate behaviour that supplies and feeds the behaviour of the narcissist/bully. Co-bullies attract the abusive people over and over again, getting hurt each time. In many cases this will eventually lead to a breakdown. It may take this wake-up call for a co-bully to question it.

Why did people think they could behave like this to me? Where did they get the message that they could treat me badly? Why didn't I have the ability to stop these people abusing me? This does not affect some people, but a co-bully will recognise it, and the above questions will resonate with them. Why did I stay in these harmful situations so long? Mary said, "the first physical abuse happened in school when I was four years of age. A teacher pulled me from the classroom, into an adjoining room on my own, and beat me with a bamboo stick several times, and at the mercy of this deranged adult, I was in shock and there was nothing I could do as a child to pacify or reason with her. I was powerless and she was the powerful one – that was the beginning of my submissive, passive personality."

It was the beginning of my shadow "self". I thought I was protecting myself, but in fact I was developing a lifelong habit that was putting me in dangerous situations. At that time, men were the head of the house, women were in second place and children had no place. It was always said that children should be seen, not heard. So maybe along the way I lost my voice or the ability to interact with unhealthy communicators, as I was not allowed an opinion. I witnessed on a daily basis children being terrorised, ridiculed, constantly humiliated and put down. The favouritism and the ostracisation, the power that authority had over you and that they could choose either. The fear of saying the wrong thing or doing the wrong thing, and the resulting punishment that would be meted out. The extent of being a co-bully varies from person to person, but I discovered I had a high tolerance for staying in dangerous, harmful situations which contributed to my pacifying and my need to put their feelings before mine. If you met me you would never have recognised I had low self-esteem. For my own purpose I am going to differentiate between self-esteem and confidence. I appeared confident. My shadow-self spent most of its time trying to keep the peace in work, home and relationship situations.

At that time a child didn't go to the authorities, it was unheard of, as society gave great scope to institutions associated with the religious orders. The state and the schools went hand in hand. It is powerful today that there are support systems available to help a person to get out of abusive situations, and to teach them that **YOU CAN WALK AWAY FROM ABUSERS** with supportive help and you don't have to stay in abusive relationships or accept abuse as normal.

We must break away from our "history", or ancestral energies, which have been passed down through generations, down through families, culture and societies which form part of how people behave today and how other people tolerate or accept the abuse. People must become self-aware and have self-love and live from the most powerful place you can on this earth, and that is your soul, your uniqueness, and your core essence.

The Feeling of being Lovable and the Feeling of being Capable

Dr Tony Humphrey's, *Self-Esteem, the Key to your Child's Education* says there are two dimensions to self-esteem: ***The feeling of being lovable, and the feeling of being capable.***

*Children with low self-esteem may be fearful of making mistakes at school because he/she may be picked out, humiliated, and diminished by the teacher. A child that is easily upset by mistakes, nervous or who is over compliant-these are indicators of a child's doubt about their **capability**.*

*The second reaction of children when their self-esteem is threatened is **compensation**. This is* evident in situations where the child is intense, nervous, spends too many hours pleasing others, is worried, or who is easily upset by any prospect of failure, or very upset when confronted angrily. By working so hard the child is trying to eliminate any prospect of failure. Failure and mistakes mean risking the disapproval of primary caregivers and teachers.

Dr. Tony Humpreys *Self-Esteem, the Key to your Child's Education* says, ***The child who shows over-control of behaviour is often overlooked and more at risk, but this can be missed by parents and others, as the child's symptoms do not upset the adult's life.***

This child's identity is tied to behaviour, unless this identity issue is resolved the child will become even more chronically insecure, and will develop people pleasing patterns. If not identified and changed, this will continue in adult life. This is the formation of a co-bully, a peacemaker, staying in harmful situations too long instead of self-protecting. Self-esteem is fragile and can be taken when there isn't an awareness of "self". A hurtful remark, a betrayal, a disapproving remark, or a cruel deed can diminish it. Narcissists can be hurtful and cruel and a co-narcissist absorbs it and feels it deeply. The only sense of control they feel they have over their own safety is by their compliance and pleasing. When this doesn't stop the aggressor it leaves them feeling powerless with little or no ability to have safe control over their life. Today we have words spinning around, but few of us actually know the meaning of what it is to have self-esteem and not to have self-esteem. To have self-esteem you have to love yourself unconditionally and be aware of having healthy support around you. When you don't have self-esteem, the effect of not having it will continue into your everyday relationships and your pattern of entanglement with unhealthy communicators. People who project will attempt to bully, dominate, control, blame, criticize, spread malicious gossip and negatively judge, they will use put downs, let downs, cruelty, silent treatment, isolation, overt and covert aggression. This is all very difficult for the co-bully, who hates confrontation and will avoid it at all costs.

The co-bully believes, *This is great, we are moving forward. This person at last is reasonable, will permit and listen to my opinion, will even compromise – but this is short-lived. You can never fully relax with a bully, as their behaviour pattern is the projection of anger, causing confusion, chaos and the co-bully's behaviour pattern absorbs it. There might be a meeting of minds on occasions but the overall power, control, and atmosphere is in the hands of the projector. Kate said, "driving into work one day, I said 'I hope she is in a good mood today', then I said 'I am in a good mood and I am not going to change that'". I went into the office and didn't allow my colleague to take my power from me. It worked that day, but projectors have a way of playing mind games. I can honestly admit I did try and keep in with her, as it was a constant struggle and sometimes it was easier just for her to have her way.*

Awareness and Support

Following professional SUPPORT, co-bullies are made aware of their pattern of reactive behaviour to aggressive communication. They will develop skills to create their observer self, step back, detach and witness negative behavior, rather than getting drawn into it. They will develop self-awareness. They will become aware of how much of their daily life is busy with this unconscious behaviour and how it distracts them from living a fearless, joyful life. Co-dependency is exhausting in body and mind, emotionally and spiritually. They will develop assertive communication skills to assert their boundaries, become confident, have self-value and to express that they will not tolerate abusive behaviour towards them. They will learn to self-love.

*Because I did not have personal boundaries, language skills, or tools to express myself, the ability to articulate it or that I would not accept abusive behaviour as normal. Nor did I have the ability to express that I was **not available** as a target, therefore I spent too long being a co-bully. I now have a freedom that I have never known. I recognise behavior when it is controlling, abusive or neglect-ful, and I do not have to compromise my happiness or safety. I am separate, detached, I don't get entangled as I witness their behaviour.*

CHAPTER 4

*The co-bully adopts passive behaviour
in an abusive situation to survive.*

Definition of a Co-Bully

A co-bully's biggest fears are conflict and rejection. A co-bully is not "consciously" aware that they are being abused because their survival in a relationship has been defined by their compliance, the supply of other's needs and trying to keep the peace. A co-bully neglects their own needs, has little self-awareness or self-love, and so is an easy target. A co-bully places no protection on him/herself; thereby, they have learnt to accept or tolerate emotional abuse, with little or no idea at times that they are in a dangerous situation. A co-bully wants to keep the peace at all costs, so when a bully initially begins their reign of terror, the co-bully will try and placate them, rather than confronting them. This is one reason why the abuse goes on too long. A co-bully empathises with the aggressor instead of recognizing the danger and self-protecting. The co-bully isn't consciously aware that they don't have to accept this abuse. Once a child has learnt to survive, function, in a situation where their primary caregivers are emotionally abusive or neglectful, the child learns through fear to defend him/herself. A child just learns to survive in a very threatening world of emotionally abusive adults. The child may become a co-bully who spends their time, energy and emotions placating a bully all through their life unnecessarily. The only way a co-bully can change is to recognise that they are a co-bully and get to the root of this behavioural pattern – then and only then can they change this behaviour with professional help. The bully subconsciously believes their behaviour is acceptable, is unapologetic, is deserving, is owed something, doesn't consider anybody but themselves, and unconsciously the co-bully accepts this. A co-bully knows it is not acceptable, but is trapped, entangled in the situation, and doesn't have the skills to exit this toxic relationship. The co-bully is fearful, but still stays in a situation which undermines their confidence, isolates them, destroys their self-esteem and in extreme (though common) situations causes sickness, and death by suicide. *Stop getting involved, STOP BEING AVAILABLE, stop trying to resolve the problem and pacify the bully, YOU OWE THEM NOTHING.*

Definition of a Bully

Bullies are perpetrators of emotional, spiritual and physical abuse. They exhibit high rates of *personality disorders*, particularly *borderline personality disorder, narcissistic personality disorder*, and *antisocial personality disorder*. A personality disorder is an enduring and persistent pattern of behaviour that negatively, hurtfully destroys and impacts many different life areas of a co-bully including social life, family, school, and work relationships. A bully who freely uses covert or overt emotional aggression, the silent treatment, put downs, let downs, isolation and mind games, or who undermines confidence, and in extreme cases, abuses (verbally, emotionally, physically, sexually). A bully controls and manipulates until they get what they want. **Fear is the bully's weapon** and way of controlling a situation. It is a way of disconnecting you from your core "SELF". In an everyday work/school/

home situation, a bully can be unaware that they are behaving in this very frightening way. Bullies behave like terrorists, and can launch a campaign of terror against the unsuspecting. If you have what they want or are in their way, or just happen to be in the same company, all hell could break loose. A co-bully may be a high-achiever in their personal school/work/life but just lack the skills to interact with this aggressive behaviour in any other way than trying to pacify. A co-bully doesn't like to resort to put downs, insults, aggressiveness or hurtful interactions. Bullies bully bullies, but they each look upon it as a challenge, it may hurt their ego and they will want to get revenge, but it doesn't manifest into fear and isn't absorbed as hurt. Bullies bully other people who are "self aware" (EA –emotional awareness). They don't get as upset, they are able to recognise that the bully has a behavioural problem and can disconnect from it and self-manage safely around the abuser.

Bullies bully the "co-bully", this is a problem. The co-bully will try and placate the bully at all costs, thinking it is their duty to make this person happy and feeling that the behaviour is somehow their fault, that they have offended or antagonised the bully and must fix it. They empathise with the bully instead of seeing the DANGER. They become entangled in a cycle of abuse. The bully will never accept the blame for the hurt they have imposed. Bullies will twist and fabricate any story to self-serve and take away the onus from them.

Co-Dependency

> "Are we enabling unacceptable behaviour in order for us to appease that person (who is causing disruption, hurt, pain, destruction, sickness) in order for us not be rejected, confronted, challenged, targeted or hated by them?"
>
> –MELODY BEATTIE

Co-dependency often involves placing a lower priority on one's own emotional needs, while constantly trying to fill the needs of others. Co-dependency can occur in any type of relationship, including family, work, or friend relationships, and also romantic, peer or community relationships. Co-dependent people are constantly in search of emotional acceptance. When it comes to arguments, co-dependent people usually find themselves the "target". When they do stand up, they feel guilty or ashamed because they don't want to upset anybody. They appear voiceless, powerless, as they don't have the language skills to express or the emotional skills to confront anyone in an aggressive, manipulative environment.

Other co-dependents e.g. co-dependents to an alcoholic can blame the alcohol but with co-dependency to emotional abuse, usually the co-dependent self-blames for causing the other person's anger, unhappiness and the relationship breakdown.

Striving Instead of Thriving

A co-bully, as a child, developed passive communication skills in their early environment to appease others and survive in unhealthy adult relationships. They may lack self-awareness and assertive communication skills to safely self-manage around EMOTIONAL ABUSE AND NEGLECT. They are co-dependent and may not understand why they are locked in this role. When you are the target of a bully or bullies, daily life is a struggle and is debilitating, frightening and isolating. Become AWARE that you don't have to accept this abuse, empower yourself to detach and exit from the situation. Learn skills to act, interact, and react with emotional abusers. Reach for people who are consciously aware and will SUPPORT, help, protect, and guide you away from the danger and from negative people. Learn awareness when another person is projecting their negative energies and learn skills not to absorb them.

A co-bully is a person who unconsciously gets entangled with perpetrators of emotional abuse and neglect and who doesn't have the skills to process or manage the aggression, manipulation, control, criticism, jealousy, sarcasm and cruelty. Abuse is not acceptable, but somewhere along the co-bully has learnt to unconsciously tolerate it. A co-bully has chosen to go through life passively, coping, trying not to hurt anyone. A co-bully should embrace themselves, as life is full of threats and their first priority is that it is never their intention to hurt anyone. I am introducing the term "co-bully" to replace words like "victim" which is disempowering, to clarify that it is a receptive role formed in early childhood and that it becomes a pattern of relationship behaviour. The purpose of this book is to make the co-bully aware that they are a co-bully, that they are unconsciously permitting this behavior, and they are getting entangled in abusive situations. Co-bullies can stop accepting bullying as "normal" and develop the skills to safely self-manage around aggression and manipulation. The co-bully assumes the role of the co-dependent self, exhibiting an acceptance of a high tolerance of inappropriate behaviour towards them. This leads to issues including being over-responsible for others, neglecting one's own needs, neglecting feelings, boundary issues, shame, guilt, and little self-love. I want this book to open up awareness that there is a path they can take leading to self-love and to safe, healthy relationships – there are places where the co-bully can flourish. Following recovery, empowerment, and getting to know yourself as this book encourages, you will become aware that you, yourself are the most influential, effective and powerful person who can awaken the "self" within and begin to flourish, grow and create. Emotional wellness and emotional freedom lead to self-awareness and self-creation.

I have to clarify the following

Every time I have mentioned being bullied, some people automatically directed their focus, concern and sympathy to the bully. – "Oh, the poor bully, they don't know what they are doing" "they are damaged people forgive them".

The co-bullies of this world are also hurt and mistreated, the only difference is that the bully chooses to continue whether unconsciously or consciously, to further emotionally damage people along their path without empathy or remorse. The co-bully who abandons or neglects their own needs takes on the role of supplying and meeting the needs of the bully. The co-bully who was emotionally damaged chooses not to further abuse, but instead will try to resolve, fix and help people, including the bully. The co-bully will stay in harmful situations for too long to the detriment of their own health and wellbeing.

Not everyone has been emotionally abused or neglected as a child, or experienced emotional abuse as an adult.

According to Dr. L. Whitfield M.D. in Healing the Child Within (1987) the percentage of people estimated who grew up with a healthy amount of love, nurturing and guidance is approximately 5% to 20%, meaning that 80% to 95% of people did not receive unconditional love, guidance, and other nurturing necessary to form consistent healthy relationships, to feel good about themselves and about what they do.

Those who didn't have guidance to self-love and self-care developed a pattern of co-dependency. Based on this there are many people who are unaware that they are co-dependent and are enacting their roles on a daily basis, some in the role of the bully and the others in the role of the co-bully.

They don't have awareness of conditioned roles or how emotional health impacts on a person's life. People's behaviour can affect a person's well-being positively or negatively. It is through awareness that you can choose to continue a life of struggling or through support and change can being to live a life of THRIVING.

CHAPTER 5

"One can scarcely imagine the terror of a helpless child locked up in the company of seriously deranged adults and at the mercy of a brutal and amoral system."

–KATHY O'BEIRNE IN "DON'T EVER TELL"

Characteristics of a Co-Bully

A co-dependent's ability to be at "ease" or at dis "ease" is affected or *evaluated* by other people's moods and it may affect their well-being. Co-dependents want balance and peace in relationships but unconsciously and consistently choose those who coerce them into experiencing abusive, controlling or neglectful relationships. The co-dependent often stays with the bully *not* out of fear of being on his/her own as thought, but their over-all attachment or responsibility for the bully's appeasement.

It is an emotional disorder that causes distress and anxiety. Their biggest fear is aggression, manipulation, being ostracised, rejection and isolation. It is a pattern of behaviour with little self-awareness that they accept or endure unhealthy behavior. They have been conditioned to please, pacify, so that they are accepted and included. The unfortunate outcome is that no matter how much the co-bully pleases, the bully will turn on them eventually. Nobody walks into an abusive relationship knowingly or consciously. Bullies at first appear friendly and "normal", or it is possible that the co-bully was unfortunately placed in a very toxic school or workplace. I have met extremely charismatic people whom I would never have believed would act abusively. Nobody accepts someone who openly abuses them when they first meet. Bullies subtly draw you in, and when you are off guard, the abuse will start. A co-bully doesn't have that alarm bell in them to warn them that they are freely walking into a very abusive situation. A co-bully is too open, loyal and trusting.

A Co-Bully

- Doesn't have the language to express or tools to self-manage in aggressive situations.

- Doesn't have the emotional ability to confront aggressive communicators.

- Doesn't have the awareness of personal boundaries or self-protection.

- A co-bully may feel they deserve it, self-blame, as the behavior has been normalised.

- Will avoid confrontation at all costs.

- Is nervous around aggressive communicators.

- Is passive, submissive, to avoid threats.

- Can interact with healthy communicators.

- When making decisions, will compromise their own values.

- A co-bully feels hurt and confused for allowing mistreatment.

- A co-bully will try to cover up the inappropriate behaviour to avoid conflict.

- Co-bullies find it very difficult to exit harmful relationships.

A co-bully just wants the world to be nice. If a co-bully had self-awareness, had self-esteem, was grounded, was aware that this was unacceptable behavior, they could self-protect. They are programmed to placate first, no matter how insulting or abusive the other person is. When they eventually realise enough is enough and want to leave the emotionally abusive situation, they find this very difficult. They are "attached" to the bully and made believe they are being disloyal if they want to leave the covert trap. This entraps them in abusive situations. The co-bully is a pacifist, and it is against their nature to be aggressive, so they will struggle greatly with responding in abusive ways, e.g. fighting or retaliation. The co-bully is emotionally vulnerable and will keep going back into the same "covert trap".

Zoning in on Threatening Moods

A co-bully will look outward to other people to seek approval, to feel acceptance and safe in company. A co-bully is fearful of verbal abuse, emotional abuse, physical abuse or that they may attract unnecessary negative attention. In a non safe environment a co-dependent prefers to stay in the background. Enjoyment may be short lived if they are targeted with sarcasm and insults. This clearly shows their happiness depends on other people's interaction and behavior. The co-bully likes to be "prepared" for negative moods and they will analyse how to respond to it. A co-bully is continuously adaptable in relationships. A co-bully must learn to stop zoning in on other people, stop reacting to other's unpredictability, have boundaries and be able to assert separateness. A co-bully must connect to their inner self, their heart, soul and mind. Our hearts tell us our true feelings, what we want to do and on what path we would like to go. Our souls tell us our true and meaningful call in life. Our minds shows us the way, guides us to live a life of love and rise above fears. Heal yourself from being a fragmented person to being whole again. Change from approval dependency to self-love and self-determination.

A Bully doesn't come Dressed as a Monster, they are Everyday People

A co-dependent has an endless pit of love, devotion, and patience, and is forever forgiving the hurt or neglect imposed on them. Hoping that this time the abuser will see the light and see how much the co-dependent accepts or loves them. A co-bully has an empathic disorder bonding through an unconscious level to resolve the bully's anger, feeling they can do it in some form. Please God, this time the abuse will stop. It is like a game; the abuser causes the pain, the co-dependent thinks in some way it is their fault. They will calm the abuse, hoping the abuser will become appeased, so they can relate to each other. It is like a contradiction; the person abused has to make the abuser feel that it wasn't their fault and will pacify the abuser.

*Eventually, the **abuser** may say this won't happen again, not taking the blame, but the abused just wants the abuse to stop, so they don't question the lack of ownership or responsibility. There is no genuine apology nor does the abuser say my behaviour is unacceptable, I am hurting someone and I must change. Therefore the hidden agreement is made, the 'covert trap' and the abusive behaviour continues. It is difficult for people who are not co-dependent to understand why a co-bully would stay with a bully, but the co-bully is trapped and believes the bully will change. Usually, this unhealthy relationship is very close, within family, school or work dynamics. It is amazing in company how the bully zones in on the co-bully like bees to a honey pot. At the beginning it looks like they are great buddies, but the two-way unconscious "covert trap" has begun. Co-bullies have little self-protection, they are passive, with very little personal power in the company of bullies, and do not have awareness to choose an emotionally healthy relationship. A co-dependent will choose the bully, work* *colleague or friend with similar relationship patterns to one of their guardians/ teachers who may have been controlling, emotionally abusive or an authoritarian figure. Their new relationship is a repeated role familiar to their powerless or emotionally neglected childhood. Most co-dependents unconsciously continue the behaviours they learnt as children at home, school or in any area of authority into their adulthood. A co-bully might have been brought up in a passive home, so they are unable to handle aggressive behavior.*

Roles Assumed by a Co-Bully

Highly Sensitive Person, Enabler/Fixer, People Pleaser, Rescuer, Caretaker, Peacemaker

Highly Sensitive People (HSP)

An HSP is a very emotional person and **feelings dominate in their relationships**, therefore they respond unconsciously through emotions rather than being rational. HSP's are more connected to their soul because they are more connected to their feelings and the feelings of others. HSPs are highly sensitive to what is going on around them and to the environment in which they live. **The NSP** (non sensitive person) **needs take priority over the HSP's needs.** An HSP attaches to people easily and feels responsible for them in many ways. HSPs are sensitive nearly to the point of exhaustion trying to sort out other people's problems. When someone verbally attacks an HSP, the HSP is unable to clearly respond, as they get overwhelmed emotionally. When an HSP is upset they lack powerful language, effectiveness, they cannot speak forcibly or directly with aggressive communicators. When a bully attacks on a continuous basis the co-bully may develop panic responses to attacks. They cannot **express or clarify what hurt them** nor are they able to sort out differences with aggressive or neglectful people. They analyse how to regain a friendship instead of seeing the danger when there has been a falling out or a misunderstanding.

Positive Energy – Negative Energy
Positive Feelings – Negative Feelings

HSP are very sensitive to other people's energies positive or negative. A HSP is highly sensitive and will zone in on people with negative energies e.g. an aggressor, they will try and calm them or if they are unhappy they will try to rectify their situation. This may have stemmed from their childhood where they may have been in negative environments and tried to rectify the atmosphere to survive. They were sensitive to conflict and mistreatment of others, therefore they absorbed other people's negative energies. The more sensitive you are, the more you will be influenced by other peoples' energies. A NSP will barely notice the atmosphere or the moods of another person, let alone act on it. That is why when the co-bully is told to "move on", they are unable to do so, because their feelings are connected to what has happened. It needs to be addressed, rectified or resolved by them whereby a NSP can move on quickly, "move on, move on" or "let it all over your head", or "toughen up" without it affecting or upsetting them in any way.

When a HSP absorbs another person's negative energy by being overly empathic or by being attached, they carry this energy as if it was their own. The HSP cannot ignore their feelings. A co-bully needs to detach and not be available when someone wants to dump their anger or their bitterness. Negative people are usually drawn to HSPs because it is their good energy they send out that makes a negative person feel better about themselves. They draw in on the HSP's positive energy. But the unfortunate thing for the HSP is when the negative person keeps drawing on their positive energy, it does not last, gradually the HSP will burn out. NSP's can ignore their feelings, they tend to disconnect or ignore their feelings, so the feelings go away. But a HSP cannot do this, that is why they analyse and try to understand why or how could a person behave towards them so badly or negatively. Sensitive people are sensitive to the needs of others and may be overly responsible for others and how they feel. NSP often aren't aware of the hurt they have caused because they are not tuned into the feelings of others. A HSP will absorb the negative feelings in a toxic environment. This may have been conditioned in childhood where a sensitive child absorbed the negative energy a prime caregiver was expressing. A HSP needs to be aware not to absorb, learn how to detach, and learn ways to release the negative energy they absorb from others.

An HSP

- Is approval dependent
- Needs to be accepted and included
- Is easily hurt by insensitive or negative personal remarks, or wrong-doings
- Takes everything to heart
- Is sensitive not to hurt others
- If they feel they've hurt someone, are actually hurt themselves
- Is usually passive until they feel safe and trust in company
- Is giving, caring and very hurt when a "friend" or associate turns on them
- Is analytical and will go over the hurt to understand it, try and reason with it, but is not very capable of expressing the hurt to the person who caused it
- Is a loyal and honest friend and will do anything to help

- Is a reliable family member, friend, colleague, and wants the best for people.

- Loves when people are happy in their company

- Where other people can shrug off insults, the HSP just cannot and absorbs them to the point of deep emotional pain

- Loves the peace of nature

Enabler

A co-bully unconsciously **enables** the bully to behave in a ruthless manner. The bully demands their way or no way. The co-bully will bear the brunt of all the bully's failures and unmet needs, and will save them from their mistakes. Sometimes to the extent that the enabled isn't aware of the damage they have done and will have moved on to the next target or destructive project. This is where the co-bully must wake up and realise they are **enabling** the bully. The co-bully clears up the bully's mess. If a co-bully highlights the negative behaviour there may be pay-back or retaliation and the enabler will suffer.

Enabling is a pattern of behaviour to avoid confrontation, arguing and "fighting" at all costs. They will absorb the emotional abuse. They may feel somehow responsible and that the bullying is in some way their fault. The co-bully will want to adjust the atmosphere. The enabler has little boundaries so it is a free-for-all. The perpetrator of the abuse is thereby "enabled" to continue their pattern of behaviour. An enabler must learn the skills required to let the bully know that their behaviour is unwarranted, but usually the co-bully is too passive. Thereby the bully's ego has no concept that they are actually ruining people's lives.

People Pleaser

In the mind of a child: *When they feel frightened or not able to manage the situation. An extreme pleaser says: If I do everything right, if I am the good girl/boy will you like me, will you stop rejecting me, will you stop hurting me?*

A co-bully can only relax in company when they feel safe and unthreatened. A co-bully is extremely sensitive to the moods of others. The co-bully must become aware of their people pleasing tendencies before they can begin their own road to recovery. There is a subconscious desire to help, solve, and change the other person's unhealthy or unfortunate status. The co-bully must recover before they can have healthy relationships with people that don't use them, abuse them, put them down and drain their energy.

A People-Pleaser

- Has an unhealthy desire to please anyone and everyone at a cost to their own care
- Is highly vulnerable to criticism and rejection
- Is naive, trusting, loyal
- Finds it very difficult *not* to help when they think a person needs help
- Will avoid confrontation at all costs
- Will ensure the other person is happy, while they shelve their own happiness
- Other people are shocked how the pleaser allows another person to belittle them or insult them in company
- Apologises even if they are not the one at fault

- Will self-harm rather than self-care

- Will stay in a harmful relationship too long because they pity (empathise) the abuser, and will stay in it even though they feel trapped

- The co-bully gives more than they receive

Jane said, "I used to say, the way some people are afraid of dogs, I was afraid of people. I was very uncomfortable around people in conflict. I was very uncomfortable around people gossiping and saying malicious things about other people behind their backs. I just wanted to work and progress in life. I never realised how unconsciously involved I was with other people's behaviour and yet I was trying to make everything look "normal". I thought it was my duty to calm people when they were angry. When people said hurtful and embarrassing things to other people (let alone myself) I always tried to pacify the situation, and change the atmosphere discreetly."

Children who suffer early childhood emotional abuse and psychological neglect, develop a condition where they will comply and please other people. Young pleasers develop a sense of abandonment, and they have little awareness of self-love, or self-care. They feel a sense of shame or guilt if the atmosphere is abusive. They are like the walking wounded, hiding their wound, as they are not important, but at all times reacting to abusive relationships.

Rescuer/Fixer

The rescuer rescues people from their responsibilities, problems, worries, and tries to sort out their problems as if they were their own. The rescuer dives in headfirst. Co-bullies tend to rescue people with problems. At times these people are able to take care of themselves, but in some way the rescuer believes they are helping. They will share advice, try to make life easier and that which involves the least amount of suffering for the person. The rescuer becomes attached to drama and people in chaos. The rescuer runs into situations which are dangerous, thankless and which would need professional help and advice. The rescuer ends up in someone else's chaos, helping to the point of exhaustion. I have witnessed the rescued people eventually emerging with little or no idea of how much help the rescuer gave, how much the rescuer worried and put themselves in danger for them. The rescuer exhausts themselves and uses up more energy than the person being rescued. The rescuer would like to be acknowledged, but the person rescued doesn't recognize what the rescuer has done, and usually is annoyed with the rescuer rather than being grateful. But the rescuer believes the person they rescued is still their "friend" so will stay involved and will rescue again the next time.

The Caretaker

The Caretaker will always want to be there for others, will want to "express" to everyone, "I am reliable", "I will help you if you are ever in trouble". As the song goes, "when you need a helping hand I will be there, I will carry you in times of trouble". People who are Caretakers look outward with the intention of seeking and caring for others. Caretakers never ask for care and usually have little understanding of self-care. The taker has a way of isolating the caretaker who supplies their needs. The caretaker is so taken up with takers they have little time for emotionally healthy people. Nervous breakdowns, panic attacks, tiredness, and burnout all are common illnesses. The caretaker's self-worth lies in their caring role. "No" is not a word the caretaker can say to people who ask for help. The caretaker usually learnt this behaviour from one of their prime caregivers, and has been conditioned to believe that the needs of others are more important. Otherwise the caretaker may feel that they will be labeled selfish and uncaring.

The Caretaker, probably learned to please an over-demanding, aggressive and unpredictable authoritarian. Little girls should be seen and not heard. Here again, choosing chaos, the caretaker needs to know that it is OK to ask for care, love, or respect for themselves. I have seen very supportive people helping and caring for other people and when it comes to their own life, it is as if they have shelved it. Their role is the caretaker's role, and that is how others see them. They choose the 'Care of Others' trap. When the caretaker needs care, usually there will be no one there for them. I have heard a person that was cared for greatly saying afterwards "I never asked her to do it".

A Caretaker

- Says yes because they can't say no
- Runs in to help without questioning the situation or truly knowing the person
- Wants the other person to be happy, even if it undermines their own happiness

Caring and being Cared for

A co-bully believes it is best to be respectful to people, but doesn't understand that not everybody will be respectful to them in return. It is important to know the difference, and not to get emotionally involved with abusive people. **Respect those who respect you.** When you care for someone it doesn't mean you give up on your own life and needs.

Peacemaker

Relationships that are regularly dismissive, sarcastic, moody, dogmatic or hostile have a major effect on a safe environment. A peacemaker will become the "go between" in an atmosphere of conflict.

A peacemaker

- Is extremely sensitive to any hint of conflict in a relationship
- Will feel it is their duty to resolve conflicts and become over-involved in trying to "keep the peace"
- Subconsciously zones in on aggressive people, believing they can help stop abusive situations. Will support the person abused, but with such little self-awareness or self-care that the bully will target them next

Fear of Rejection

Rejection hurts profoundly and causes serious psychological sense of loss and pain. It is why bullies reject and encourage bystanders to reject, to inflict their power and diminish their target. Bullies thrive and gloat when they isolate a person. A bully's aim is to crush and manipulatively insinuate that there is something wrong with the target. "Whispers in the gallows". The fear of rejection is disproportionate in the co-bully and that is why they keep trying to please and keep in with abusers. On some unconscious level a co-bully believes they are unworthy, unlovable and they really have to work hard at maintaining relationships. Unconsciously, the co-bully sets themselves up for rejection continuously with emotionally unavailable and unpredictable people. **Ostracism is a threat to the four fundamental needs of a person**; the need to belong; the need to self-control, self-protect, the need to have self-value, and the need to have a meaning in life. A threat to any one of these will cause personal stress and pain.

Powerful Vs Powerless

The powerless are in no position to question, offend or antagonise the powerful. This experience is relived on a daily basis as an adult if dominated by an authoritarian in school or home. The co-bully believes by complying, the other person will be agreeable in return. A co-bully will try to placate anyone who threatens them, to ward off aggression. It is the pattern the co-bully has learnt to survive and keep safe.

CHAPTER 6

The oppressed become the oppressors

Characteristics of the Bully

An emotional abuser has developed a pattern of negative behaviour and isn't consciously aware that it is unacceptable or harmful. They seek those co-bullies who will link in with them subconsciously and supply their shortcomings. The co-bully will unconsciously seek a bully for their approval, inclusion and non-rejection. Bullies project their feelings of anger and **seek those who are available to accept and tolerate their anger and harmful behaviour.**

Bullies/Takers/Narcissists have an unbelievable sense of self-importance and the co-dependent must enhance this. They are self-centered and can make demands with a smile on their face. A smile that the co-dependent interprets that they cannot refuse this person or they will get abused, insulted, or subjected to a rant that may turn into a full rage.

An abuser feels that if the co-bully takes their abuse, they deserve to be treated badly. A bully will bully if they get away with it. There is no abuse without the abused. Bullies will be "against you" rather than "for you" in a relationship, no matter how close the relationship is, the underlying current is that there are always put downs, and you are in the wrong, they will never support you when you need them. This is a very obvious trait in a manipulator.

- Bullies have a personality disorder and lack empathy
- Bullies are devious and behave ruthlessly when they target a person
- Bullies have to feel they are in control
- Bullies resent success and happiness in other people
- Bullies have a strong sense of entitlement and superiority
- Bullies are very jealous and begrudging by nature
- Bullies use terror tactics and have no sense of embarrassment
- Bullies are duplicitous and malicious
- They freely project and vent their anger onto other people
- They are volatile when angry
- They have no respect for anybody else
- They have a means to an end, to get what they want
- Bullies freely use put downs
- Bullies change the rules to suit themselves
- A bully appears/pretends to sympathise but really has little feeling for anyone else
- A bully can be seen to be normal once they are getting their needs met
- A bully demands constant attention, admiration, and can be overpowering in company
- A bully is quick to verbally attack any co-dependent who tries to reason with them

- A bully craves feedback, wants to good points about themselves from others
- Envy/Jealousy eats them up, they hate if someone appears more successful
- A bully believes people are jealous of them, fantasizes about being successful, attractive, intelligent, without actually working/studying for it
- Bullies love being in a position of power, they exploit others for personal gain
- Bullies are arrogant, have a strong sense of self-importance, will make someone else feel inferior to hide their low self-esteem
- They hate criticism, but will crush others viciously
- A bully behaves in the way that gives them the most attention.
- People are surprised to learn the level of abuse projected behind closed doors
- Bullies will ignore a speaker to diminish them

Taker

The Taker zones in on the caretaker to have their needs met, the taker usually uses methods such as forceful demands or manipulation. Takers are usually moody, cause scenes, embarrass the "other person" into meeting their needs. The taker can act overtly, or covertly aggressive, and will keep at the supplier until their needs are met. The taker appears quite dismissive, has an air of self-importance, displays arrogance, is ruthless and doesn't care who they impose on or who gets hurt. They play hot and cold and have no awareness or concept of other people's boundaries. They gatecrash or bulldoze their way in a relationship and isolate their target to be available for them at all times. There is little acknowledgement or appreciation for what the caretaker does, they take what they want and can leave without any thanks. The taker begrudges caring for anyone.

Rebel

Rebels are in an immediate response mode, ready to pounce and react aggressively to people and situations. Rebels consider themselves to be non-conformists but rarely have a profound, strongly developed ethos. In fact, they have spent little time on personal development. They are domineering, aggressive, and will constantly react to people in an argumentative and often critical manner.

A Controller

A Controller will do anything to exert power and diminish others. They use covert, overt, devious and aggressive manipulation to get compliance. A controller is possessive, oppressive, powerful, jealous and domineering. The controlled will initially feel wanted or valuable because the controller is charming, but they quickly dominate and render the controlled powerless. This will be enforced using careful tactics, limiting access to places and people. By this stage, the controlled has unknowingly walked into a trap of being possessed, used and abused and does not have the skills to exit this toxic relationship. The bully's need to be in control causes great distress. The bully who is out of control is obsessed with the need to control.

Narcissist

Bullies seem to glide through life, taking everything they can along the way. They manipulate, use and abuse the most vulnerable people and they get away with it. They are extremely devious at wriggling out of acknowledging or taking ownership of their behaviour.

Narcissists envy others and become obsessed with another person's ability, success, popularity or their position in a workplace. Many narcissists are obsessed by self-aggrandisement, entitlement, status, money and power, and will go to any lengths, disregarding everyone to get what they want. They are envious of others who seem to have an abundance of everything. Narcissists crave adulation and praise, and create a public persona of their falsely superior self. They really strive to publicly present themselves in a very praiseworthy way. On the surface, in everyday (distant) relationships, they may appear likeable. They can turn the charm tap off or on. However, in intimate relationships, the real "narcissist" surfaces – Street Angel, House Devil. The narcissist interacts displaying (overtly and covertly) envy, arrogance, superiority and entitlement. They cover up and protect themselves from rejection, sarcasm and embarrassment by over-reacting with contempt or outrage. A narcissist will exploit others to serve their own demands and needs. They are highly skilled in controlling, using and diminishing others.

Verbal abuse is the main tactic of the narcissist but always with an underlying threat of punishment or violence. A narcissist is very quick-tongued and will leave a person spinning from a verbal assault. A narcissist will belittle a person behind their back through malicious gossip and put downs, and will round up the herd for the unsuspected attack. A co-bully will be left reeling and wondering when and how did all this start. This strategy is going on behind their back and the bully is fully armed with bitterness and hatred. The situation becomes unmanageable. This abuse is grossly underhanded and is the main weapon of attack. It completely disarms and disempowers, it is how the bully establishes dominance and superiority. It is used to gain control, diminish and isolate the co-bully, who takes on the subservient role. The situation becomes dangerous and unsafe.

A Narcissist

- Is oppressive, domineering, tyrannical, critical and harsh

- Will use tactics e.g. hounding or badgering the target to submit

- They will dishonor what is important to you, who you are and what you do

- Will overpower you and take ownership of your "self" and your resources

- Exploit people to get what they want

- Has no empathy, causes major emotional pain, disruption and destruction. Does not care or understand who they hurt or what hurt they cause

- Is unwilling to recognise or identify the feelings and needs of others

- Has a destructive jealous streak, will ruin, sabotage relationships, careers

- Has an air of authority, haughtiness, importance

- Has a false sense of grandiose importance, will exaggerate achievements, will expect/demand obedience and full attention to their needs

- Craves power, success, admiration

- Wants to be seen with powerful people

- Will covertly demand or expect special treatment

Negative Emotions

Guilt

Manipulators are experts at making a co-bully feel guilty, "you did something wrong, it is your fault". Manipulators make you feel like you owe, or you never do what they want, that you are selfish, that there is something wrong with you. It is an underhand way of keeping a hold on you. It is very difficult to escape the guilt trip. Feelings of *guilt* instilled in our minds at a very young age reinforce our repression and acceptance of this imposition. It is a tool to oppress, suppress and repress a co-bully. **Guilt ties you to the bully and is a weapon used by the bully.**

Shame

A bully's shame is the co-bully's shame. When bullies behave appallingly, the co-bully is attached and feels somehow part responsible. They unconsciously get entangled and tied into their shame. They feel as if they are part of that shame. The bully tactfully ropes them in, rendering the co-bully to feel sorry for them or feels the need to cover up or retrieve the behavior. The bully uses tactics to off load the shame. They find it difficult to detach and assert separateness from the bully's behaviour. Prime caregivers may have blamed the child for anything shameful, this is then in the psyche, which adds to the amount of shame already felt. A child who was diminished emotionally or spiritually will develop low self-esteem and will feel ashamed for any mistake or imperfection. They are tied into relationship shame. The co-dependent is filled with shame and fear when he/she does not please the bully.

Worthless

A bully will keep up their tactics until there is a loss of self-love or self-value. Bullies have a great ability to make a person feel that there is something wrong with them. After an attack a person may feel ostracized with a profound sense of not belonging. A target may become frightened and won't know who to trust. The target may be unable to form further friendships, or have trust in school or work colleagues.

Having been an excellent worker and contributed well to the workplace, a target will no longer feel of worth or that they belong, but will be made feel like an outsider, a person who has done something terrible in the workplace. A bully loves to make a person feel like a problem, like they are lacking. A co-bully will, after a bullying episode, feel powerless, frightened, and after a couple of episodes will be walking on eggshells. Everything they do is watched, criticized, interrogated and put down.

Anger/Rage

Emotionally angry people are full of unexamined rage that has never been resolved, usually from their childhood. They live their life projecting aggression and hound or seek those who are available to take or accept their aggression. This is the covert aggressive trap. Somewhere along their path the bully has learned to respond to everything through anger, which grows into emotional violence. It becomes part of the bully's personality and their pattern of behaviour.

Unfortunately, non-aggressive people are going to cross their path, with little skill to self-protect around this vented anger. They are always on the verge of anger and the destructive part of this is that the bully will make every effort to cruelly crush another person's well-being. Other people are lucky that they can walk away from this rage and have the skills to self-protect.

A covert aggressive person's behaviour can go by unnoticed for some time. They want to come across as a nice person. They hide their angry and destructive behaviour until they feel they are in a place where it is acceptable, or the co-bully can't manage it. They appear helpful but subtlety use put downs. They create doubt, uneasiness and chisel away at confidence. Bullies have a strong need to "control" others and are very dominant and threatening in their communicating behaviour. A bully has a great fear of losing control over a person or place. The church, state, parents and teachers ruled children through control, fear and intimidation. Bullies still openly practice authoritarianism which instills fear, displaying (overt, covert) negative anger as a means of communicating. Bullies need to learn how to communicate safely without projecting fear, but through respect, openness, and celebrating the capabilities of people.

Disconnected from Their True Self

Bullies are disconnected from their true self, and everything they do is an act. They love negative drama where they are the successful person and someone else is seen in a poor or bad light. Some bullies are not consciously aware of their hurtful behaviour and see it as a means to an end to get what they want. Bullies hurt and put down anyone that allow them. Bullies are drawn to people-pleasers, sensitive people, caretakers, givers and enablers. When their ego is in control and on a high the bully may abandon the co-bully or treat them very badly. Bullies are expert manipulators and make you believe they can't be done without. They play a game of hot and cold, changing the goalposts to have continuous trapping into their game. If the person is moving away they will turn on the charm tap. That is why the co-bully must become aware and stop accepting abusive behavior. Not everybody takes this abuse. Bullies openly believe they have the permission to condescend, put down, hurt and abuse. They love trouble, gossiping and instilling fear. They love having a fan base and a circle of admirers. The bully loves having a co-bully on their side, because a co-bully is sensitive and a people pleaser. The co-bully must realise when they are in a danger, the bully will blame them if bullying is questioned. The more they give in to the demands of the bully, the bolder the demands get. The co-bully may invest a lot of time, love and patience in this covert trap before understanding it is abusive.

Take Control – Seek Professional Help

The only way you can **take control** and stop this dance of abuse is to realise you are either a co-bully or a bully and **get professional help**. The co-bully puts him/herself in the path of emotional abuse. But also, the co-bully is unconsciously enabling this unhealthy, emotionally abusive behaviour by accepting it. The co-bully believes they are helping the bully but the only thing the co-bully is doing is prolonging the abusive behavior. Someone has to say 'stop' and get professional help.

Covert aggressive bullies have learned to *cloak their anger,* but have not learned to control it in a healthy way. They may appear not angry, but there will always be an undercurrent, an understanding that all is not well. This inner rage, fuelled by not being in control, not having their way, will lead them to create difficulties. If you are the target of a group of bullies or been ostracized, you are in a very vulnerable and probably dangerous place. Authorities with people in their care need to manage this abusive behavior before it gets out of control, more powerful, and where a co-bully will suffer enormously under this regime of terror without support. It needs to be recognised as unacceptable abusive behaviour immediately.

CHAPTER 7

*When it comes to violation, destruction and hurt the only difference
is the Abuser's choice of WEAPON, whether the weapon
is Physical, Emotional, Sexual. All have lifelong
consequences for the person abused.*

Emotional Abuse

I am *not* using the word "victim," as in my experience the co-bully is targeted, so I am using the word "target". The word 'victim' labels the co-bully as being helpless, directing fault and blame. Institutions have been negligent, have failed in their responsibility, turning a blind eye to children and adults who have been targeted under their management or care. Even with professional help it is very difficult to appease the bully. So why do organisations expect a targeted person to resolve situations with the abusive person on their own? A target needs professional support from people in paid, responsible positions who must support or stop the reign of abuse in their jurisdiction.

Emotional Abuse is a weapon used to diminish control and hurt another person. In some cases it is the intentional withdrawal of love, inclusion or friendship. The use of fear, vibes, humiliation, covert, overt emotional aggression, silent treatment, oppression, dominance, control, verbal assault designed to frighten, isolate or undermine the self-esteem of their target. It may be frequent or occasional. Emotional abuse can be verbal or behavioural, and will leave the abused crushed. Emotional scars last longer than physical scars, both will leave deep psychological issues. If a child, through conditional love or no love develops a pattern of conditional love, they will learn to neglect their own "self" love. Emotional abuse is often dismissed by adults because the wounds are not visible and the adults aren't "consciously aware" and haven't self-examined their own behaviour, so the abusive cycle continues. It is astonishing to hear adults when a person is being psychologically/emotionally abused, say "get over it", "move on, move on", "forgive the abuser", "toughen up", which in turn doubly abuses the abused and allows those in responsible positions to neglect their duty of care. **Targets are not looking for sympathy but they are looking for understanding and support in their coerced circumstances that they have been forced to endure**. A manager's job is to manage the care and protection of students or employees, in places that claim to have a Dignity Policy in place.

Emotional abuse will fester in the subconscious, and it emerges in everyday responses of an emotionally abused person. It is a learned behaviour to respond in a threatening world. The unfortunate thing for the emotionally abused is that they have deep scars which are held in their heart, when they have little support or understanding of this **chronic distressful emotional state**. Emotional pain hurts deeply, is held in the core, will affect the emotionally abused in their attempts to function healthily on a daily basis, and will stunt their emotional growth, which will impact negatively on all areas of their self (SPECIAL). They will be unable to function and partake in everyday events.

Emotional abuse will leave the target feeling guilty. This is all internal, so the emotionally abused may appear to be a "normal" person, but is surviving in a very hurt place. They haven't taken the time to self-examine, taken time to heal or to get to know their loving and safe place in this world. They haven't learnt the skills to act, react and interact in a safe environment. An emotionally abused child, unless healed, will continue their passive receptive, communication into their adulthood.

Until a person recognises that they are a receptor, they will never be able to start their recovery and self-empowerment. With support and a therapist they can begin to "self" love. It is more painful to continue life being available for abuse and neglect. With good therapy a person can stop this conditioned behaviour and be free from accepting abuse as normal or that they "deserve it".

Emotional abuse is extremely difficult to identify because the condition has been normalized. The co-bully believes they have a relationship but it will be discarded with little or no thought or empathy. The co-bully has been unconsciously set-up to be available or take their anger or abuse. Usually, over a long term of abuse, the co-bully will have to run from or leave the situation to preserve their own physical and mental health.

It is thought that a person is only abused if they are abused physically, but emotional abuse is more common, secretive, subtle, more devious than, and as harmful as physical abuse. In today's society it appears more acceptable as usually it goes on "behind closed door", or its "domestic", or "in-house" or there are "policies in place". People in distress are afraid to speak out as they feel they are causing a fuss or attracting unwanted attention, or who do they go to, who will listen, who will understand their situation? With emotional abuse there is always the underlying threat of physical abuse, when the bully is angry or in a rage, who knows how far they will go when they are out of control. Emotional abuse is frightening, bullies have a way of projecting fault, and a co-bully will do anything to appease this bully. When a co-bully is in this trap, they really don't know how to get out of it. They don't want to upset the bully, firstly because they never wanted to do anything that would go against the bully and secondly they feel no matter what they say the bully will be unreasonable and they feel any interaction will lead to conflict. In a conflict situation the bully has the power. In a workplace/school this is very frightening, because in front of other people, especially people of authority who can give the bully what they want, they can come across as reasonable people. The authorities turn a blind eye to abusive behavior and at times just don't deal with it. Again, emotional abuse makes a co-bully question themselves. *I have heard people in Management and in Employee Relations say, "they never complained through the correct channels, so there is nothing I can do" or "it is just a personality clash".* So they just stood by and did nothing to resolve it. The bully is so manipulative and powerful, they have a plan in place, e.g. a promotion, or your job, or they are just motivated by jealousy, or because you are there, so in hindsight you can see that you were in their way, or you had something they wanted. They also use you to make you appear lacking and make themselves look better.

The Emotional Abuser gains more power and control until they have a right to dominate you, humiliate you, to constantly tell you that you have done something wrong (as they will never say you have done something right), they use put downs, silent treatment, covert or overt aggression until, unknown to yourself, you nearly have to ask permission to say something, or before you are allowed your opinion, because anything you say could cause conflict, a big bust up, a flare up, and you will have no idea how it started. You are in the company of someone who five minutes ago was smiling, now they are angry, deranged, and they make you believe that you caused this.

Emotional Abuse doesn't just "Go Away"

The abused gets weaker trying to appease the abuser, while the abuser grows stronger. It takes a lot of strength and energy out of the abused, trying to continuously appease, but the abuser gets more confident, more powerful and gains more control. Emotional abuse gets worse over time as it erodes a person's *self-esteem*, confidence, energy and trust in their own judgment. It is similar to brainwashing – it can cause a target to question reality and their own sanity, which leaves them at the mercy of, or relying on the very person who is abusing them. Like other forms of abuse, emotional abusers strive to overpower the other person – **the one with all the power has all of the control.**

Emotionally abused children will have a distorted perception of how to form healthy relationships. Children, by nature, are fragile, vulnerable and less powerful than adults, so it is only natural for a child to try to act in such a way that they will not get hurt. Children learn to respond to conditional love by taking on the role of being the pleaser and will go through life looking to others for acceptance, inclusion, and for approval of their self-worth, usually from emotionally unhealthy people. They will confuse approval with love and will spend a lifetime looking for approval from others, confusing it with love. When the unhealthy love is unreturned the co-bully will believe it is their fault. This will form into a pattern of ill-founded relationships which will instill in their psyche the idea that there is something wrong with them. This will also make them cover up more, please people more and attract even more abusive people. It is a covert trap and they will need professional help to stop this abusive cycle.

The hidden wounds are not visible, so nobody suspects there is anything wrong with an emotionally abused person, and they are told to toughen up. It could lead to a life of little self-love and struggle on a self-destructive path. Abusers have a covert way of inflicting guilt. The co-bully has learnt to be voiceless, takes second place of importance and accepts the abuse for the sake of the family, society, school, or workplace. A co-bully who is vulnerable in the company of a bully is persuaded to think of the abuser first and to forgive them. In company a co-bully will take second place to a bully for peace sake. This gives a message to the bully they are of more worth and to the co-bully that they are of less worth. They engage too much energy and attention on the abuser, rather than focusing on self-healing. A co-bully deserves to be respected, cared for and loved in a healthy relationship.

Discipline

Discipline brings back memories of dark days when adults made a lot of threats to stop a child from doing wrong, making the child fear their behaviour was bad. For decades, parents, teachers, prominent members of Irish society and clergy ruled children through fear and intimidation. Behaviours such as shouting, beating, hitting, criticising, threatening, ridiculing, and scolding were commonplace in homes, schools and churches. Children grew up instilled with unhealthy methods of communicating and relating to other children and adults. Children were oppressed in a system of abuse openly acceptable in society, called corporal punishment. Authorities had the power and the powerless, vulnerable children were targeted. From this stems the receptive reaction to abuse which is the co-bully's mindset and the aggressive reaction which is the bully's. The co-bully adopts passive behaviour in an abusive situation to survive the abusive threats and is quiet, non-assertive, unable to express themselves in a threatening, unsafe place. A co-bully cannot physically or verbally confront a bully. So in a work/school environment it looks like the co-bully is getting on fine, but they are, in fact, struggling to self-express freely. They will give the rewards to the bully so they can be left alone and not harassed. *The co-bully will hold back on their own development just to keep the peace.*

Formation of the Emotional Abuser's Personality

Emotional aggression is covert violence. This behaviour is learned when the child is exposed to primary caregivers who were dominant, cruel and aggressive. The child learns or copies emotionally aggressive behaviour to get what they want and to survive in the world they are beginning to be a part of. From then it is all-out war, taking and manipulating to get all they want. The child learns they will never be listened to; it is intrinsic in school, homes, and communities, "do as I say or there will be consequences". The child will learn to get what they want through underhand warfare. The child will become manipulative, appearing normal but will manipulate to get what they want, as they know the dominant adult in their life has little or no interest in the child's opinion, that there are conditions to being loved, therefore they have no understanding of self-love. Confrontation will only bring abuse to the child. Unfortunately, the child, when they become an adult, will bring this way of behaving into their workplace, their home or their social circle. Bullies are experts at using the tone of their voice as a method of controlling. They will either shout, show rage, or use equally covert aggressive methods such as silent treatment, ignoring and refusing to acknowledge a question or by not responding to it. Usually, this is followed by a condescending look to make you feel inadequate. Bullies use words to hurt, intimidate, belittle and to oppress. They can verbally attack in an instant, which leaves the receiver reeling or frightened. Bullies will continue with this verbal assault to wear a person down and to get what they want and make the co-bully powerless.

Begin to Assert Separateness from the Controller

A bully has a personality disorder that inflicts suffering onto another human being without understanding it, or having empathy or remorse. The relationship rules or dynamics following the first erratic outburst, threat or conflict will lead the way to how the relationship will continue. It may be an over-reaction, blow up, or an exaggeration of mistakes but it is the beginning of the control and shame tactics. At this time **If The Co-Bully Does Not Express** that this behaviour is unacceptable and it infringes on their safety and well-being then there is an unspoken agreement to the bully that they have a **FOUND A PLACE** where they can without unquestioning freely and without punishment impose unacceptable behaviour. It will become the atmosphere of how they will relate to each other. The projection of abuse will escalate and progress further because now the aggressor is gaining more power and control. The bully's negative behaviour is now normalised and accepted in the relationship. From this time on it will become a struggle of survival for the co-bully. A bully will see the co-bully as a source or convenience where they can behave as they want. The co-bullies needs or feelings will not be recognized. The co-bully is conditioned to reply or respond to each demand of the bully. They need to embrace new skills and realise YOU ARE NOT OBLIGED TO and it is not necessary to respond or interact with anyone who is over powering you, controlling you or making you nervous. When you have developed assertive skills you will be able to self-manage. But until then, the beginning of the self-realization journey is to be aware that you are not attached to this person physically but psychologically. You can detach from them. The first giant step is to begin to assert separateness (emotionally), start separating yourself from their line of control. Give yourself SPACE and familiarise yourself with your own personal space. Detach and stop having empathy towards them and "look" at what is happening practically rather than through your emotions. The bully's tactic is to isolate, disempower the co-bully who will become hyper vigilant and in constant response mode. Take time alone to process what is actually happening, not what you've been told is happening and do not respond in "panic response". You are an individual and just because you walked into an unsuspecting control trap, you have the right to exit it. Just because you were tied to them in the past you don't have to be tied to them in the present or future. Begin to question yourself, "what do I want", what is "safe or right for me" rather than "what do they want" or "how can I keep them happy"?

Detach, rather than responding and getting deeper entangled with the manipulator. The more you respond to them, the deeper you are getting involved and the more difficult it will be to extricate yourself. You may feel you are pacifying them but you are actually disempowering yourself and giving your power to them. Stop looking to them for approval, approve yourself. It is not your responsibility or it is not a "forced" connection to supply and "to be there" for them. Express your boundary and articulate it. When you are caught up on an atmosphere of blame for "everything", step back, **until and if** they self-examine or they recognize their unpredictable behaviour is affecting your well-being and take ownership, and be willing to change, until then remember it is not a safe place.

It is a friendship not an ownership, it is an engagement not an entrapment, it is a relationship not a dictatorship, you have a right to do what is best for you and you can walk away. A relationship is a two way connection of healthy communication where each party feels "trust and peace" and "safety without hurt".

You may believe or they may have made you believe that you are "connected" to this person through love or friendship. It becomes "disconnected" when the bully's behaviour becomes abusive, controlling and now there is no respect for boundaries but you are available to accept when they need to "dump" whether it is their anger or their chaos. They will overpower you and over take you to "be" all and everything to them. If you do not provide their short comings, their demands and if you are not responding, they will manipulate you e.g. "I thought we were friends" or "I thought you loved me", this is emotional blackmail. It is not your place, your duty to provide or to be there for them. Do not permit them to live their life through your energy, your empathy or your resources, a relationship is **two separate healthy communicators who communicate together** to support, love and respect each other with healthy boundaries. You are in control of your own thinking and you can say YES OR NO.

CHAPTER 8

*"Love knows that you exist and cares for your existence with
a new birth of the heart, you will see a new world."*

–Deepak Chopra

The first step in **recovery** from emotional abuse is to evaluate and
understand your relationship patterns, your close-relationships, your
relationships with others, but especially your self-relationship. It is your
first step to begin to discover your true "self". Through therapy you begin
to see how your false "self" or co-dependent "self" subconsciously took
on the role of trying to survive on a daily basis. How it began to appease
another's anger and get entangled and caught up with unhealthy behaviour.
Examine with a qualified therapist where you began your co-dependent
"self" and get support to become self-aware, change, self-empower and
prevent you from accepting future abuse or neglect as normal. Connect
to your true "self".

Signs of an Emotionally Abusive Relationship

- You often feel afraid. You avoid certain topics for fear of anger

- You feel that you can't do anything right, your opinion is not listened to

- You feel trapped, overpowered and struggling

- You don't know how to be treated well, therefore accept mistreatment

- You feel you don't fit in. You feel emotionally vulnerable

- Aggressive and critical tones humiliate you

- The bully treats you so badly that you're embarrassed your friends or family might see it. The bully ignores or mocks your opinions or accomplishments. You have no control over how the bully mistreats you when you alone or when in company

- The bully blames you for his/her own abusive behaviour

- The bully is jealous and possessive. The bully controls where you go or what you do

- The bully keeps you from socialising, mixing with other friends/ colleagues/family

- The bully limits your access, and constantly checks up on you

- The bully is in your space and your personal boundary is not considered by them

- You feel your responses and interaction are in panic mode

Forgiveness is for the Person Abused, *Not* the Abuser

The second step in recovery is self-forgiveness and self-love. Self-forgiveness releases from the subconscious the embedded emotional hurts. The origin of the problem is *the way you were conditioned to think, the psychological terror you were conditioned to endure, the inability not to have been able to say "stop" and self-protect.*

To understand what actual forgiveness means for the person abused, forgiveness is easier to say than actually do. Sometimes it is so difficult to understand what actually went on. It can be difficult to explain what you felt or why you feel so bad. Deep emotional pain hurts and it can crush you emotionally, mentally and physically. It can take a person from a place of belonging to a place of exclusion. You feel you don't belong in your former life or you feel you don't belong in the life you are now part of.

A co-bully is isolated, frightened and in a place they thought they would never be. The people they trusted have manipulated and turned on them. They have inflicted suffering and irreparable, unwarranted hurt. It is very difficult to heal and let go of the overwhelming pain. Forgiveness can be especially confusing when you are told to forgive the abuser. The focus is on forgiving the abuser when deep down you don't believe the person is entitled to it. Forgiveness doesn't mean condoning or excusing the abuser's wrongdoing. This is where it is so important to let go of that attachment to the abuser(s), and stop trying to analyse why they abused you. It is very difficult to understand "WHY" and how a bully could have been so cruel, so heartless, when the bully might have been a family member, close friend or colleague. **A co-bully must stop trying to understand the bully's behaviour.** Just know they are abusers and you must detach and go to a safe place away from them. The only person the co-bully must forgive or will get to understand and change is themselves with the help of a qualified therapist. It takes the co-bully a long journey to disconnect from the abuser. Release yourself from the anger or resentment you may feel towards them, that is self-forgiveness, it is the only forgiveness you need.

Self-Forgiveness

Forgiveness is for You

The person who is deeply hurt by another person's hurtful and damaging behaviour. Firstly you self-forgive for not being able to manage your "self" safely around this person's manipulation, lies and deranged behaviour. It is healing your pain within, reconnecting to your "self" and **releasing your "self"** from their anger and resentment, negative energies or any attachment you may have or feel towards them. You are not responsible for their behavior, it is nothing to do with you, you just happened to be in the wrong place with the wrong person. A co-bully must learn to self-care, be self-gentle and let go of trying to make everything right. The reception and acceptance of abuse was a learned behaviour in childhood that continued into adulthood.

You Forgive Yourself

You don't need to reconcile with the abuser, and you don't have to condone their actions. You "free" yourself from accepting their abusive behavior as normal. A misleading statement is that "healing requires you to forgive the abuser", which in itself is most destructive because it is keeping the abused attached to the abuser and in the cycle of their abuse. You **forget** the abuser and you self-heal.

For the first time in your life, think of yourself and put self-love first. The abusers move on to the next target and you are not a passing thought to them. Do not spend time thinking of the abuser, only be aware they are an abuser, and do not invest anymore of your precious time on them. It will be difficult when the person(s) you invested so much love or trust in has wronged you and shows no signs of remorse or empathy but over time, with self-awareness, self-examination, you will understand and will have the skills to detach.

The abuser has no right to forgiveness, such blessings, such goodwill can only be a reward for good behaviour. Release yourself from judging their behavior and leave that to the Higher Power whom they will face one day. The only forgiveness and help required now is self-forgiveness, self-empowerment and self-love. Emotional abuse doesn't leave physical scars, but there are deep embedded scars in the psyche. The co-bully needs to detach from the abuse and realise they didn't have the skills to ward off the abuser, or that there wasn't a supportive system in place to support and help them. The person abused must not waste more time now thinking of 'what I did wrong', and 'I must forgive them'. **Break free from the cycle of abuse**.

Try to come to terms with what happened instead of wishing you could go back and change it, which you can't, and realise that you don't have to hurt in the present, because you've been hurt in the past. Detach from their abuse and assert separation of yourself, remove yourself from the abuse and the abuser. It is their abusive behaviour not yours. Hand it back. **It is empowering to draw a line, separate the past from the present. Become aware that in time you can learn to leave the hurt in the past and move forward without their abuse in your heart or mind.** Through meditation you can learn to change memories of bad experiences to under-standing they were lessons in your past. You can change your thought process to look at it as a learning experience and with new self-awareness CHANGE, focus on the ability to see love and feel love in your everyday present.

When you hold on to hurt, injustice and the fear of re-occurrence it pre-vents you from living a healthy fulfilling life. Co-bullies become so wrapped up in their past hurts and fears that they can't enjoy the present. They may become anxious, depressed or disconnected from themselves and from others. When you cannot express hurt outwards you suppress it inwards which evolves as depression. When you aren't able to process, release or understand these feelings you are the one who suffers. The person bullied only becomes slowly aware of the suppression of unresolved feelings when they start their journey of emotional healing. The amount of abuse taken piles up until one day the soul just cannot take it anymore. The co-bully may have a breakdown, which is a sign that enough is enough, this abuse has to stop. It is a "wake-up". Emotional over-toxicity is the cause of emotional, spiritual, mental and physical illness. The surrounding herd mentality can inflict on a co-bully the idea that the co-bully must shut up and put up. The group must appear normal, and *a co-bully's feelings are secondary and are not important or taken into consideration.* Usually it is a person in authority (who hasn't self-examined) who encourages the co-bully to move on and who really hasn't taken the time to support, investigate or resolve the situation. They have little or no understanding of the **chronic emotional distress** the co-bully is experiencing.

I don't comprehend why society keeps telling the co-bully they must forgive the abuser. This actually keeps the bully in their circle of thoughts so the co-bully will never recover, because they have to think about the bully. **Again, they are made believe that the bully deserves more thought than themself.**

The co-bully must begin their journey of self-love and self-care. When a co-bully begins to connect to their love they will become aware there is a Higher Love who is there to love unconditionally. A person in recovery must let go and let God in, and understand there is a power higher than them. This situation has become unmanageable, so hand over the burden. This will take some time to understand. It is not the abused person's responsibility to have to think of, let alone judge the abuser. The abuser has done enough damage, the abuser has done wrong.

A healing citation the co-bully may say: *"Lord, I am hurt, but I don't want to carry this burden with me anymore. I am handing it over to you, you are Divine Love and it is you who will have to meet this person. It is between You and the abuser. I am not expected or able to judge this person. It is a great relief to hand over that burden to someone who is stronger than you. This is empowering.*

The co-bully will become aware of a place that is love, and they will understand that they don't have to be in a place of fear or punishment anymore. When Love becomes your focus, rather than fear, when you know you are just a part of a bigger supremacy everything else will fall into place. Our core will become love, and all that inflicted hate and misery will not be inside but handed over. When you are set **free from the slavery of co-dependency**, of focusing on others for acceptance, approval and love, then others will not be able to diminish or hurt you. When you connect to self-love and you become aware of conscious and unconscious behavior, you will transform from a lower consciousness to a higher consciousness, life will become more understandable. Your life will have a purpose, the power will be within you. Rather than pleasing and seeking the approval of "unconscious" people, and their forced compliance, you will be focused on self-love and your spiritual journey. Your life's disappointments will become life's appointment to love and care for your own life.

"To thine own self be true."

–SHAKESPERE

You may have spent years in the role of being a co-dependent and depending on others for love, approval and validation of how you feel about yourself, whether you feel good or bad. When you are a caretaker, a peacemaker you may have lost touch with your true-self and are now dependent on others opinions for inclusion and acceptance. You may find yourself in a state of turmoil. Depending on others for evaluation will lead to inner chaos as people's opinions maybe manipulative, unpredictable and changing, playing hot and cold or making you feel good or bad. People who are not "conscious" of their behavior are dependent or co-dependent.

Our souls need TRUTH and until we are in a state of self-truth our minds will be in turmoil. It is truth that heals. Otherwise there will be disorder and disharmony leading to self-punishment which leads to spiritual, emotional and mental illness. You must have faith to lead you out of the chaos. FAITH is the surrender to become aware of truth from the support of a conscious person to guide you to supreme healing and supreme unconditional love. Surrendering is to know when we need support, when our core-self is unconsciously upset, is unbalanced or is out of control. We are not in touch with our real feelings (LOVE) therefore to return to our TRUE SELF we must seek guidance from conscious support.

> *"Personal decline is the result of deception and false friends.*
> *Recovery is the result of truth and genuine friendship."*
>
> –READINGS FOR RECOVERY BY C B KEOGH D.D., PH.D

Life has a great purpose for each and every one of us. When we have been hurt, abandoned and abused Love will be your healer and take the burden from you, which you must hand it over. We don't have to seek outside approval or put ourselves in danger for love, it is already in us in abundance. Recognise that you are powerless in this situation, let go and trust in Love.

CHAPTER 9

The abusive cycle.

Related Personality Disorders

The Abusive Cycle is a common occurrence in relationships involving people who suffer from Clinical Personality Disorder, *Antisocial Personality Disorder, Avoidant Personality Disorder, Borderline Personality Disorder, Dependent Personality Disorder, Histrionic Personality Disorder, Narcissistic Personality Disorder, Obsessive Compulsive Personality Disorder, Paranoid Personality Disorder, Schizoid Personality Disorder,* or *Schizotypal Personality Disorder.*

Negative Behaviour

Anger, Rage, Aggression, Manipulation, Violence

Aggressive people may not be "consciously" aware of their negative relationship with and around anger. Aggression or manipulation for them has become normalized. They have little self-understanding, lack the ability or capacity to express anger in a safe and acceptable manner. They are unaware of what is acceptable or unacceptable. Are they aware or do they question how much anger can the other person take, accept or feel safe in? Will the target fear and loose any sense of control for their safety in this toxic or dangerous situation? People who have an unhealthy relationship with anger often find that it surfaces as fear, which may lead to physical ill health, mental or emotional problems. It can create an angry personality, the *aggressor*, who few people have the skills or ability to confront safely. It can create the *receptor* who unconsciously tolerates anger, has an intense fear of anger and will avoid confrontation at all costs. The aggressor or manipulator will seek those who have difficulty with confrontation or assertiveness. This can lead to emotional issues such as stress, fear, nervousness and hyper vigilance. A child may have learned fear and mistrust because their prime caregivers were angry or emotionally unavailable, unpredictable and unhealthy. This follows into adulthood, when the adult is unsure or lacks a "healthy model for communication" with others. The aggressor may lack self-awareness in their ability to control their anger towards another person(s) or the receptor(s) lacks the ability to self-manage when they witness or are in the company of anger.

Uncontrollable, anger in an adult is anger that hasn't been dealt with from their childhood, which continues into adulthood as rage and or as an "angry personality". In a home or workplace, any person should not direct their anger or rage towards another person. Open, supportive communication must take place, and issues need to be resolved healthily. Anger that isn't managed healthily, unexpressed, suppressed, will promote outbursts of aggression and this makes it difficult for the receptor to express a safe boundary. A receptor has issues with **creating a safe boundary** – usually a sign that this person was conditioned in childhood and learned as **a vulnerable child that they had no right or safety in saying "no"**. When they did try and express a safe boundary they were not listened to. Children are taught how to be treated and how to accept mistreatment which continues into adulthood. Physical, mental, or emotional abuse may have affected the child and now, as an adult, they say "yes" even if they want to say "no", just to keep the peace. Subconsciously they are reliving the fear and trauma they experienced as children. Fear that has been embedded in their psyche and now as an adult, have never learned the skills of creating or expressing safe boundaries. Anger is a primary emotion that is a critical part of our survival system. Anger is an emotion designed to alert you that something is wrong and that you need to address it, or change it, but it doesn't give a license to abuse. In a home or workplace, professional, effective communication is paramount. A good manager manages, doesn't engage in bullying or doesn't tolerate it.

A person should not feel fear or feel threatened in a home or workplace. Every person must have their dignity and abilities respected. If a manager has an issue with an employee it should be handled in a private, professional manner with a witness, not through public humiliation. A manager must support an employee under his/her leadership to perform to the best of their ability. A manager must never "gossip" with one employee about another employee behind their back.

Are people consciously aware of their anger and the affect it has on people around them? I have seen people who are angry, witnessed overt, covert aggression and violence. Is aggression an acceptable part of life, are you weak if you are not aggressive? Are you playing victim if you can't display aggression or express your boundaries? Why can't you say "stop" and remove yourself from aggressive situations? Who is listening?

It is amazing in this day and age, that emotional aggression, manipulation, and the silent treatment are still widespread in workplaces, schools and organizations. Even with bullying policies in place, such as dignity at work, someone can still intimidate, threaten and diminish their fellow students or co-workers. Anger (a strong feeling) is an expression that shouldn't be intimidating, but it is an element in communicating to express that you feel a person has wronged you and is an alerting mechanism for them to let them know that their behaviour is not acceptable.

Co-bullies are unable to focus their anger at the abuser so many will turn it inwards, leading to depression and self-harm. There is a sense of "no self". If the co-bully had strong self-esteem, she/he would be able to say, loudly, "I did nothing wrong", "it's not my fault" – unfortunately, the co-bully self-blames. Co-bullies need to feel their anger, name it, and direct their anger at the abuser. (in a safe and supportive place).

Following abuse the co-bully suffers and the emotional pain imposed is deep. The feelings of failure, self-loathing, loss of control over their lives and the fear of attack are so intense. They tried everything to comply but it was of no use, so they are left feeling worthless and isolated. These feelings are authentic and it is important to know them, understand them but **not to act on them**. Remember, you want the bad situation to end but not your life. You may feel trapped, with no apparent exit but with new self-awareness and with support you can find one.

The co-bully must leave this toxic situation immediately and seek support from people who have self-examined in a protective environment. It may take knocking on a few doors, but positive help is there, as there are "other people who have been in that trapped situation who broke free and are now living an abuse-free life. A co-bully needs to learn new life skills, i.e. "break free from the aggressor and recognise their danger".

Bullies are angry their whole lives and will project their anger onto anyone who will take it. Bullies' anger goes beyond the boundary of anger, bullies have rage. This is why you can feel the vibes of rage which can be very intimidating.

There is a further difference between anger, rage and violence. Anger is a strong emotion, a feeling that cannot hurt anybody. Rage and violence are some of the behaviours that negatively express that emotion. Many people do not know how to control their anger until they reach an explosive point. Aggression causes unnecessary hardship, unhappiness, fear and sickness. This anger may be triggered by the current situation but the bully may also be tapping into a well of old rage. Rage stems from anger, in that, in certain cases where there is anger present, the ultimate push will create an out-rageous occurrence. Rage tends to be expressed in an atmosphere where it is acceptable and normalised. Bullies believe they can get away with it, they do it openly or in a very subtle way; an outburst, then a smile on their face, which leaves the target entangled and bewildered. People in a rage are extreme and are very frightening. A passive communicator cannot under-stand how they express their rage so openly. They are so explosive you don't know what they are going to do. They look like they are possessed. There is always the underlying threat that violence may follow the rage.

Rage is an expression of the anger the aggressor has inside, it is an explo-sion of built-up anger that is boiling up and anyone in their path will feel the wrath of their anger. At this stage, they are out of control and their anger overtakes their ability to be reasonable. The bully's purpose is to hide their aggression, and also to create fear and doubt. The covert narcissist makes their victim feel like they are the one with the problem, whilst projecting an innocent, angel-like persona to everyone else. They make their target look bad and do their best to destroy their reputation in order to enhance their own deluded, false sense of self and their distorted view of the world. Narcissists have **no empathy** and therefore have **an invisible secret**, and use it as an advantage to manipulate those around them.

CHAPTER 10

*You must heal within with unconditional self-love, self-protection,
return to a state of unity only then can you think of moving on.*

Recovery after Abuse

**The world is full of threats and anger, but our life experience might be
more compassionate and gentle if we have self-awareness. The self-belief that we don't have to accept relationship abuse as normal and we
can break free from our role as "receptors".**

Abuse is a violating and a devastating experience for anybody to suffer.
Someone without your permission has diminished, deceived and damaged you. They have gone on with their life with little or no awareness or
acknowledgement of what they have done. The most hurtful thing is that
you probably trusted this person, and it could even have been someone you
really loved and invested yourself in unconditionally. But there is recovery
after abuse, and there is a life after abuse.

Remember that the abuse is not your fault and you are not responsible.
You mustn't blame yourself, or feel you should have tried something else
to change the outcome. You mustn't feel ashamed, guilty, or think that you

have failed. The first step is to clearly accept that the relationship is toxic and dangerous and that this person has an aggressive and manipulative behaviour pattern. You must do something to change or exit this abusive relationship, you must self-protect and remove yourself from the abuse. Recognise that you will never change an abuser. Abuse isn't caused by the receptor doing something "wrong" or feeling that they are not lovable, it is a behaviour pattern perpetrated by the abuser. **They will abuse anyone that will accept it and will target those who are available.** Abuse can come in many forms, psychological, mental and emotional. It can include hurt, humiliation, control, threats, diminishment and degradation. If the person continuously makes you self-doubt, feel bad about yourself or makes you feel unworthy, it is an abusive situation. If you are afraid to do things because of a spoken or unspoken threat of punishment, physical violence, psychological violence or other "revenge", the relationship is abusive. Don't stay with anyone who abuses you. It is dangerous to stay with someone who is abusing you. It will eventually break you down, and make you give up on yourself.

The initial ability is to recognize that **abuse is a FACT**, a reality – a hurt. Someone has hurt you. It may be a small hurt or it may be an unbearably terrible one. Some hurts are so deep rooted that it may seem impossible to heal this root, but in time with love and understanding, this root can change, grow and blossom. Most people's issues can be traced to hurts, going all the way back to primary caregivers, culture, ancestral, or religious concerns; parents, siblings, extended families, teachers, friends, or colleagues. Hurt once experienced is embedded in our subconscious, we have to go to our origin of our hurt, acknowledge it, understand it, love and heal it.

Through psychotherapy, examine it, address it, heal it and move on then, but only then, when you are ready. If you don't go back to the origin of your "self" forming role of a co-bully, you will not fully understand, or believe that you are now able to move on. The most important task you must do is to connect or find your "self". The only person you must think of at this fragile stage is you, you must be kind to yourself, you must remove yourself from the abuser, lock them in a box away from you. What you are looking for is peace, peace within. Society's herd mentality is fearful of anyone that wants to break away, so unconsciously society wants you to stay in the group. When you are healed, when you self-forgive for not being able to stop the abuse, when you self-love, then you will realise that the abusers are in darkness. Forget the "abuser", just get out, and self-heal. **You forgive people for your benefit, not for their benefit.** Think about your own life, your own painful situation that needs healing. No matter how bad it was – no matter how bad it *is* – Self-forgiveness and self-love will change your world. When we process and understand what is actually happening, with support and awareness we can change and stop accepting it.

When it is emotional abuse it is a deeper, and a more hurtful pain. It is an all consuming pain. We remember the pain, the hurt, and we carry it with us everywhere we go. It consumes our life and saps our energy. It creates a wall between our true "self" and the loving intimacy of our "self". This causes health problems. It not only causes us to be unhappy, but can ruin the ability to have a self-relationship, or healthy relationships with others. It distracts us from life and makes us reluctant to embrace new things and people. We get trapped in a cycle of fear, reacting to abusers and accepting hurt, we miss out on the beauty of life. A lot of "self" work and self-examination is required, the road to "self" discovery may be painful but you will reap the benefits. With self-forgiveness and self-love we begin to heal, it is the BEST GIFT you will ever give your "self" in your life.

Personal Boundaries

A good personal boundary is basically an ability to say "no" or stop when we feel our space has been invaded. When another person pushes themselves into our space and it makes us feel uneasy. It is a moment we should follow our gut instinct and let this person know they have crossed the line and we must step-back, examine and revisit what we feel is happening. A co-bully has learned to put other people's needs first, this is where the pattern starts. A co-bully must become self-aware, say stop, learn to self-protect, have safe boundaries and put their safety first. A co-bully has no real boundaries, and this leaves them available, open to abuse and struggling to maintain a sense of self.

CHAPTER 11

We are spiritual beings having a physical experience, rather than physical beings having a spiritual experience.

Healing – Self Compassion

When children have been emotional neglected or abused, when their primary caregivers have been unconsciously unable to provide a place of well-being, safety and unconditional love. It leads in adulthood to abuse, addiction, rage and a severely damaged, diminished sense of self, in fact a lot of people have a sense of no "self". They have been traumatised, trying to survive, trying to cope with adult threats and have lost the ability to self-love and to self-bond unconditionally. They have connected through their defences and act out from a defensive position on a daily basis. Love has conditions to be met.

We must re-connect to our inner self and our authentic feelings. When we are not in touch with our feelings we are dis-connected from our true consciousness. We allow other people who are not connected to their feelings to dump their unwanted negative feelings and we absorb them. This leads to co-dependent relationships.

Following supportive therapy, examination of past hurtful experiences, finding a new self-awareness and being surrounded with "conscious" support, a person will begin their journey of self-love and self-forgiveness. When you have taken time to self-heal, when you have self-compassion and self-love then, and only then, can you know your "self". Being disconnected from self-love is the cause of emotional, mental, spiritual and physical distress and illness. The compulsion to look outwards, to run out of ourselves for intimacy and inclusion will lead to feelings of restlessness and chaos. Searching for unconditional love outside of ourselves and never finding it. You can only unconditionally love another and another can only unconditionally love you, when you unconditionally love yourself. A holding which is love knows the world is full of threats, can react to fear, defend the "self" from threat or abuse, but doesn't become fear, bitterness, anger, jealousy, or a destroyer of love.

When you have acknowledged your wound and you have self-forgiven for not having the awareness or the ability to stop the abuse initially but you can now, then you are making progress. When you haven't self-love, it is a very hurtful place to be. Not only from the point of the lack of self-love, but because when you don't know how to self-love, you **attract unexamined people who don't know how to love you** either. Abuse happens when a co-bully who doesn't love or understand enough to self-care or hasn't got the language or tools to say stop. When you are disconnected from your "core" you are disconnected from self-love. When you open the door to self-compassion you open the door to self-healing. When you empower yourself to self-love unconditionally, then and only then can you move on. Don't listen to anyone who tells you to move on before this point, because they are not "consciously aware" and you will move on but only to repeat and accept the same unconscious hurt and abuse over and over again.

You begin to self-protect probably for the first time, an invisible but a protective aura about your personal space. Children are vulnerable because they cannot protect themselves and this will continue into adulthood until you develop the skills to assert your boundaries. A co-bully must express a requirement of safety in their interactions with other people. A boundary will express your personal space and safety and will keep others from controlling your space.

Become aware of your conditioned behaviour, your reaction to life and, with professional support, you can become aware and CHANGE. With this new self-power, self-awareness, at last you can learn to love, care and protect your "self" from a safe place. You actually will connect to the "real" you, probably for the first time in your life. You can react to other people consciously, you won't be addicted or have a compulsion to over-care, please or put your "self" in the path of anger and cruelty. You won't ACCEPT OR take on their punishment or oppression. You will interact with people now in a healthy conscious way. For the first time, you will be able to have healthy relationships or be aware when a relationship is unhealthy. **You begin your journey of becoming co-dependent free.**

Most of us were taught, conditioned to think of the other person first, to put another person's needs before our own. We had compassion for others but we never felt it or thought about self-compassion. A co-dependent must stop the addiction of constantly zoning in and reacting to other people's unpredictability, their cruelty and hurt.

When you are repeating the same pattern of the acceptance of abuse from others, your inner "core" is crying out, but we have been so conditioned to keep striving that most of us don't hear or understand that call for self-love. That wound from the inner child is calling out to be healed and to learn to stop repeating the same abuse, for you to change and find your "self" self-protect and self-love unconditionally. Emotional abuse, once experience as a child, will be in your subconscious. Emotional abuse is one of the cruelest and most profound damages, and you will re-enact it over and over again in your adulthood, until you come into consciousness and change how you learn to respond to that abuse. A cruel deed or remark from a parent or prime care giver will affect a child more than a hundred hurtful remarks from a stranger. You may have become a bully or a co-bully and have lived your adult life, responding in either way, but it can stop, you can change, heal and self-love unconditionally.

You can change from a place where you accept abuse or neglect as normal. You may be subjected to intentional or unconsciously projected abuse. But abuse is abuse, it is felt. You may have had close contact in your childhood with someone who instilled these negative, unhealthy relationships patterns. It can go back generations and it can be ancestral. The world has a long history of spiritual, emotional and physical violence which is still going down through the generations and not being healed. It can get passed down and on from one family to their next generation. We react to anger thereby becoming attached to anger. Emotional abuse can be verbal, behavioural, overt, covert, passive, seldom or often. You are misrepresented as a "victim" when you are an emotional target, a target for anyone's or everyone's anger, because you did not have the skills to love care and protect yourself and there wasn't a support system in place. It reduces the child to the point of feeling that they are unworthy of friendship, of love or kindness. It makes a person feel like they have to justify their existence. Embrace your life, heal and thrive. The hurt will always surface in relationships until you self-examine, heal and develop conscious behavior awareness.

Empathy

Empathy is the capacity to feel emotions; it is the ability to understand, to be aware of, and to be sensitive to. It is the capacity to experience thoughts, actions and difficulties of people in need without it having to be communicated. It is having an emotional capacity of feeling how another person is feeling. Empathy is an emotional response to another person's emotional state. Empathy is the core of our sense of morality and our ability to interact compassionately. The existence of empathy in a person is a sign of having conscious behaviour awareness.

Apathy is not having the empathy or care for another human being. It is being disconnected to the distress or pleas for help. The non support of a "loved" one is believed to inflict greater hurt than that of anger or hate. The "laissez faire" attitude while using it as an opportunity to gain is aversive behavior to some people. Author *Leo Buscaglia* is quoted as saying "I have a very strong feeling that the opposite of love is not hate-its apathy. It's not giving a damn." *Helen Keller* claimed that apathy is the "worst of them all" when it comes to the various evils of the world.

Empathic Personality Disorder: The co-bully over empathises and is personally affected by another's emotional state. It leads them to ignore and suppress their own personality, needs and priorities in order to cater to the more demanding bully. Empaths zone in on other people's need of care and never question the validity of this care. Empathy is the emotion that leads co-bullies to dive into situations without protecting or caring for themselves. It is empathy that entangles co-bullies with bullies. *Bullies use the co-bully's empathy as an opportunity to gain while at the same time use it to exploit, diminish, disempower and to violate.*

Affective empathy is being affected by another's emotional state. The co-bully has a strong ability to sense other people's emotions and this may affect their own emotional state. If the other person is distressed the co-bully will feel the distress. If the other person is angry the co-bully will zone in and will try and rectify their mood. Unfortunately affective distress will increase the feeling of personal distress in the co-bully and if it isn't managed and recognized it will eventually lead the co-bully to entanglement, psychological exhaustion, an emotional burnout.

Cognitive empathy is the ability to rationalise another person's situation and understand what they are feeling. Having cognitive empathy will enable more open communication and a better understanding of their situation. You may be able to respond rationally e.g. to a disaster rather than responding emotionally e.g. being upset.

Emotional empathy (compassionate empathy) is when a person is well-attuned to another person's inner emotional world, will respond and want to relieve the person of their distress and help to change their circumstances.

Lack of empathy is the disregard of another person's emotional state. Suffering can be witnessed without feeling any concern. Bullies feel no remorse if they cause hardship and suffering to those close to them whether it is intentional or not. **Lack of empathy is the main weapon of a bully**. The co-bully has an empathetic personality disorder (over empathising) and zones in on a person who doesn't have empathy. In the meantime the bully manipulates and their only "secret" concern is to use it as an opportunity to self-gain. They regard others as pawns, and a way to obtain self-gratification. They seek pleasure by manipulating those nearest and eventually may even destroy them. They use vulnerability as an opportunity to gain and at the same time inflict their vented anger and resentment. Bullies will not support in a time of need and will take pleasure in abandoning you. Bullies have no interest in anybody else's survival.

Dark side of empathy – Bullies do not have the emotional capacity to have empathy or sympathy for their targets. Lack of empathy in a relationship leads to dangerous personal situations which include levels of abuse, cruelty and betrayal. Bullies can act charming and charismatic, for a time but can quickly change to dangerous personal attacks leading to severe injury, loss, or even death. Empathy is a requirement to be a conscious loving and compassionate human being. Following a bully's attack a co-bully may suffer post traumatic stress disorder. This is seen sometimes as "stealing the soul", as the experience is so devastating, it leaves a person questioning their own "self". Therapy will be required to support the co-bully through this disturbing experience. When a co-bully believed or supported a bully the after attack of this betrayal is immeasurable. It causes immense suffering and will require support to the distraught "self" to reconnect to any sort of belief that there is a "safe place". The worst feeling of devastation is that the co-bully trusted this person. **The absence of empathy is the inability to love, care for or truly relate to another human being. It is the bully's secret weapon**. Its absence denotes an emotional and mental disorder. It also denotes a lack of awareness and respect for other people's safety, individualities and boundaries. Unfortunately in today's material world empathy will hold you back, it is far more rewarding to be cunning, to abuse, to deceive and to self-gain.

Let go and Let God

When you are in a very hurtful place, you must learn to let go and let God, and believe you have done the best you could at this stage to survive in life. Just reflect and know that you are loved unconditionally. Life is full of threats, and some of us just didn't have support, self-protection, personal boundaries or emotional skills to handle abusive people, and by being pleasers put ourselves in danger a lot. You must admit to yourself that your life is out of control, and hand it over to the Higher Power, who is there to love and care for you, as we have distanced ourselves from our "self" and the Higher Power.

When the people you thought loved you and cared for you have turned away from you, abandoned, rejected and abused you, you must believe you deserve to be loved, know that the Divine loves you. Focus on Love and not on the people who have hurt you. Know you can love yourself unconditionally. Learn the lesson, become aware of your "self", get skills to self-manage around negative people. Begin to tap into the wonderful universe which unfolds every day in front of you, but you are so blinded by hurt and pain you cannot see it.

Start each day and breath in love to your heart and be completely wrapped in love. The divine light will fill you with love and all that fear and pain will begin to lessen. **Switch on your own inner light of love and connect to your self-love.** If someone has really hurt you, hand that burden over and believe that they will meet their Maker and judging them is nothing to do with you. This is possible only when you have begun your healing journey with support and when you begin to understand the purpose of life.

Let go of the stress (it does take time), the constant chaos in your mind, and hand it over, just try it and you will be amazed how over time, you will be relieved of a lot of that pressure that we brought on ourselves because we were co-bullies. The conditioning of trying to please everyone, attracting abuse, no protection, putting your health, your love and good feeling of your "self" last. To see the world through the eyes of an awakened conscious being is so much more calm and appreciable. You are not constantly striving, but at peace and happy with the gifts of life. You will find and see little miracles every day, when you bring peace into your life, it is a much more loving place and less threatening. You are not on your own. You have someone to protect, guide, believe in you and support you. The Divine will love you, will not abandon you, and will give healing, understanding, faith when you need it. Open your heart to abundant life, a spiritual life and a life lived through love not fear.

Understanding what Letting Go is

By this time enough people have told you "let go", "move on, move on," but up to now you were unable to, you didn't know how to. You began your journey of self-awareness, of finding yourself, becoming the observer, in shock at the realisation of what was wrongfully done to you, and of how much abuse you tolerated in the past. You are now learning new ways of healthy communication and interacting with people and becoming co-dependent free. But you still can't understand how could someone you trusted, helped, confided in, most likely liked or invested your love in, how could they do this to you? How could this person you thought you knew, unashamedly hurt you so badly and so deeply without the tiny bit of remorse. You must stop trying to understand the behaviour of relational abusers but just be aware that they are.

Emotional pain is very deep pain and it erodes the very core, essence of your being, of your reason for being. It is a very lonely place to be. The person you loved and trusted has gone on with their life with no empathy or understanding of the deep hurt and damage they have caused. You are locked in a state of loss, of pain, of not being able to understand. This is the stage where you must reach into that very core part of you that is love, that is kindness and re "connect" to your sacred self. When you see or think of the aggressor, you must let go, release and hand over that pain to the Higher Power.

It is because of this emotional closeness, there is emotional hurt, emotional damage, because you invested your emotions, love and care in this person who now has turned on you and has hurt you relentlessly. Be aware that you could try and analyse it for the next thousand years, but you will never understand why an abuser did that to you. An abuser is a damaged person who has unconsciously chosen to continue to abuse. An abuser doesn't consciously care who or what, and unfortunately the abused is usually someone who has a close connection and who was available to accept this abuse. Therefore the term co-bully represents someone who is co-dependent unconsciously. A co-dependent must now begin self-care skills and break free from the abuser and think of their self-preservation first. The abused must detach from the lethal line of abuse and cut it. A co-bully must be aware that this connection is harrowing and soul destroying. A bully needs professional help and nothing you do will change them only prolong the abuse. A co-bully must search deep within and get the tools to extricate themselves from the attachment to the abuse suffered and the abuser. This is an exceptionally hard thing to do, an exceptionally hurtful place to be. But the co-bully must understand the hurt, detach from it and, having commenced their path to healing recovery, must realise that this is the final ceremony to let go and move on. A co-bully must self-embrace that they have survived in a very difficult and a very hurtful place. But they must take their first step to self-love and begin a life of self-growth. We must let go of all the hurt and imposed punishment in our hearts and **connect to our own real love within**. When we connect to our true-self, we are love.

Self Awareness

When a person has experienced a profound emotional hurt and may be unable to function "normally", they may have a break down. When in such a dark place, a cruel place, when they feel they can't go on, their true "self" will call out and with support help them to see the light again. It is like being hit by a fast train, their belief system doesn't make sense anymore. There is a huge sense of "no self", a sense of being worthless and not belonging. The only hope is that they meet their "teacher" on life's journey when they most need them, who will support and help them out of this sadness. They begin their journey of awakening and getting to know their true "self". It is the "self" crying out to be rescued. When a person is in an awakened "place", when they look back they will see help was put on their path but they were in such a chaotic place they couldn't see it.

The only way forward to get out of this place of suffering is to self-love unconditionally, to have support and positive professional help. At this stage a person probably has endured a long time of accepting abusive behaviour, coped with it, but never understood that they don't have to accept this or that they can break free of the abusive cycle. You are physically on this earth to learn a lesson. The same lesson will happen to you over and over again until you learn the lesson. Co-bullies want to please, to pacify and it will become a pattern of accepting abusive behaviour until you learn the lesson and stop this acceptance of abuse. You are on this Earth to connect to the Higher Power, to love your true "self", to be loved and to love others. N D Walsch, in "Conversations with God" says "The soul has come to the body, the body to life, for the purpose of evolution. You are evolving, you are connecting to your "soul". You are using your relationship with everything to decide what you are becoming.

This is the reason you are here. This is the joy of creating "self", of knowing "self", of becoming, consciously, what you wish to be. It is what is meant by being "self" conscious. Unfortunately, we have been conditioned to think that the false self is the real self, which it is not, the false self is the ego self and it will never be satisfied. If you could know your inner self, your true self, your spirit, all is asked of you is love. Everyone should live their life through love every day. Unfortunately today, most people are disconnected from them "self", there is no "self". Many people are living their life through fear. The "ego" self is the demanding self. Striving and never arriving, always wanting more. Living in the wilderness and living their life through their ego. Unfortunately, a lot of the "egos" have learnt to live their life through fear, which manifests into anger. They live their life through anger instead of love. People have been conditioned to act unconsciously, so the majority of abusers are not "conscious" they are abusers. The co-bully is not "conscious" they are accepting abuse, and it may take them a long time to realise, to be conscious that bullying is abuse and it is not acceptable. We have been conditioned, taught by religions and by society to turn the other cheek, to forgive and forget, so really nobody is learning the lesson to self-love, these statements encourage and permit abuse to flourish and continue.

In today's society we are being bombarded with what our "self" is. We are brainwashed to love ourselves, but that is the physical self only, the ego self, so the majority of people are focused on loving their false self, struggling, because the ego loves fear, feeds on a person never being at peace, therefore never being still, and just being. People may have lost touch with their true "self", which is all love of "self", which is love, care and protection. Your Higher "self" wants to be at peace, but your "ego" wants to keep you in state of fear, chaos and turmoil. Commercialism is today's slave trade, luring and getting people hooked on trying to "fix" themselves, therefore a person is never at peace with them "self", the ego demands hatred of self, people have lost touch with inner peace and love. The pressure to be physically beautiful, stunning, is so much an external pressure, while a person at peace is a beautiful person to be around. Self success is more rewarding than material success.

The union of Self and Spirit is a blessing in life. You must see your "self" as love before you can relate to anybody else in love. When you live your life through love, it shows the way for the soul to grow. As you grow, more of your spiritual path is revealed to you, and when you truly find love, you find yourself.

So why do bullies enter our lives, hurt us, try to destroy us? Relationships are a tool to learn to know your "self". However bad your situation is at this moment, it is where you are supposed to be in the Universe. However bad you feel about the person causing you pain, that person is the right person you are supposed to be with at this time. This person is the right person, because he/she is a mirror of who you are inside. When you are struggling with a bully, you are struggling with yourself. It is a lesson to face a conflict within. Every fault you see in them is a denial in yourself. The mistake some people make is that "someone" out there is going to give you something that you haven't connected with your "self" which is love. If you haven't connected to your "self", your love, you cannot connect to another's love.

When you are forced to "let go" there is great loss, but it has been made impossible for you to carry on in the same capacity. You must know your life has gone out of control and you just can't manage it anymore as it is. You must stop being hard on yourself and permitting other people to be hard on you. You must detach from abuse and abusers. You must take time to be kind to yourself, to connect to your deep self-love. That is all the Divine Love asks of you, to live your life in love and through love. When you have found your inner self, your true self, then you can move on and only then can you **care for** the rest of the world. But until you are at that stage, you are not able to care for, love and protect others.

Break Free from Co-Dependency

What is a Dependent?

A dependent is:

- A person with a substance addiction e.g. alcohol, drugs or other

- A person with an emotional health disorder

- A person with a mental health disorder

- A person with a compulsive disorder e.g. gambling

- A person with a chronic illness

What is a Co-Dependent?

A co-dependent is:

- A person whose main focus is maintaining their relationships and who take on the role of being the fixer, no matter how neglectful or abusive the relationship is

- A person with a pattern of accepting unhealthy and neglectful relationships

- A person with an empathic personality disorder

- A person with an approval dependency disorder

- A person with an anxiety to be accepted and to have a sense of inclusion

- A person with a strong compliance pattern

- A person with an intense responsibility for others and attaches themselves to person(s) who themselves take or feel little responsibility for themselves or their actions

- A person who is a people pleaser

- A person whose security and happiness is attached to another person's moods

- A person who is highly sensitive

- A person who communicates passively with an aggressive communicator

- A person who almost asks permission to make personal decisions so they don't attract anger

- A person with low self-esteem

- A person with an extreme preoccupation to make the other person happy

- A person who cares deeply for another person but disregards care for themselves

Conditioned love in childhood may give mixed messages to a child, who craves love, inclusion and acceptance. A child may develop a one way method of communicating i.e. outwards, trying to please the adult and may develop hyper vigilance in response to adult demands. A child needs support and love no matter who they are or what they do. When an adult has an unhealthy method of communicating with children, it will render the child unpredictable and unstable in their responses, as they are trying to comply with the unpredictability of the adults in their lives. A co-dependent places the other persons' needs and emotions in a higher priority or response before their own. The other person in the relationship is more important than their self-relationship.

To detach and enable change from the role of co-dependency as it is related to emotional childhood dysfunction, a person may work with a therapist, to examine their past to determine where and how they began their role of co-dependency. Working with a therapist means working together to get to the origin of the root of this behavior, understand it, acknowledge it, accept it and with a therapist's support commence to become co-dependent free and *not be available* to be abused or accept abusive behavior as normal.

Codependent Behaviors

- Will abandon their own emotions and will over empathise with *the other person's negative emotions*. It is how they relate to another person in a relationship

- Feel they have to give to feel their "worth" in a relationship, leading them to over "give" of themselves and their efforts

- Don't have self-protection boundaries

- Stay in a relationship because of their feelings of loyalty in a friendship/ relationship even though the relationship may be dangerous or unsafe to their well-being

- Feel guilty or nervous if they feel they are being over assertive

- Find it uncomfortable and feel uneasy when they receive compliments or gifts from others

Codependency stems from somewhere in your past, you were either a witness to or were part of a codependent relationship. Through these situations, it was expressed that your needs, wants, or emotions weren't of importance or of worth. Healthy communicators weren't available to listen or to support you and your needs. This could have been family, school or cultural. You may have been in an aggressive environment whereby an adult or an authoritarian demanded or threatened you to meet their needs. This may have instilled in you that you had to keep in with their teachings or their way of behavior. This taught you as a child to suppress personal emotional and physical needs as you developed so that you would not be targeted, rejected or abandoned by that person or group. It may be how you learnt to survive and to deal with the trauma of the situation. A percentage of adults that children interact with have little "conscious behaviour" awareness. When the child leaves this dysfunctional environment, he/she may continue this pattern, within school, friendship, work or other relationships, and it may then get passed down through generations.

Treating Codependency

To receive healthy, positive SUPPORT from people who are "consciously aware" and who are emotionally healthy:

- Individual talk therapy

- Education and awareness about the condition and how it affects you and your relationships

- Group talk therapy

- Learning tools to *not* accept abusive behavior.

- Learn to focus on your "self" and your personal growth

- Learn to detach from other people's unexamined negative "emotions" and focus on your journey

- Join a supportive group where you can be with like minded people, e.g. if you like art join an artist group, if you enjoy writing join a writer's group. A place you can express yourself safely and a place of encouragement for you to grow

Trying to comply and fit in with another person or group is unpredictable, and will create anxiety unless that person or persons is/are healthy communicators. You will tap into their unexamined negative emotions which will lead to personal chaos. One minute you feel you are accepted and feel at ease whereby in the next turn you could be the target of put downs, negative personal comments or exclusion. A co–bully must first learn awareness of self-love, self-acceptance and stop zoning in on others for a sense of belonging. This is difficult to begin with as you may have spent years complying with the demands of more demanding people first. This has to stop. This is an addiction to belong. Unfortunately some of us didn't have strong supportive networks e.g. home, school, community or social groups. With unsupportive groups we began to rely on "others" to feel acceptance, inclusion and a sense of belonging. This puts the co-dependent constantly in unstable, unreliable environments, always reacting and responding to the chaotic needs and demands of others. A co-bully must begin, when they want to make sure the other person's needs are met first, so they *"will be permitted to fit in"*, STOP and say *"I accept myself, I love myself"* and stay emotionally detached. You can still be in company but will only accept fair treatment, emotionally healthy communication and respect. Stop looking for permission or direction from other people, you are more than enough your "self". **I am enough, I have enough.** Everything or every answer you need is inside of you and you will not find it from another person that has not self-examined. (excluding qualified therapists or people who have self-examined).

When you find yourself with that obsession of zoning in on a "person" or relationship and you are analyzing it over and over, "what did they say" or "what did they do". When you are caught up in preoccupation with the opinions of others, when you are made doubt your own opinions or decisions and when you are being manipulated to value their opinions over your own. When you are confused and can't make sense of what they did or how you reacted to what they did. This is time now to begin your change, detach, **SHIFT YOUR FOCUS**, re train your vision, because **a healthy relationship would not put you in this position.** This urge to understand why they did something hurtful, just realize they did and you need not interject their "unexamined negative emotions" anymore. It is also very difficult to express or communicate what you want to say, or how you feel because you are made feel your opinions are of less importance and minute compared to their more important "life". This anxiety and uncertainty because this is a "friend" or maybe a "colleague" and you thought you were in a safe place of trust and acceptance. Now this relationship, the emotions have changed and you are feeding into their negative emotional unpredictability. You may have a feeling of resentment over lack of acknowledgment of your personal investment in helping them. Instead of zoning in on a person (group) (relationship), become aware and redirect, refocus your thoughts to your "**LIFE**" and begin retraining your thoughts to actually nurture your growth rather than on the whys and where of an unhealthy relationship.

This unlocks you from your role of co-dependency and begins awareness of your own personal journey. This emotional instability affects your thoughts which in turn affect your mental health and your ability to relate to life and people. Returning or finding your emotional wellness and emotional stability returns you to your core "self" which is your core mental health.

CHAPTER 12

Making the unconscious conscious

–M.Scott Peck

Conscious and Unconsciousness

How and where do we learn that the way we behave is labeled normal or acceptable behaviour? Where is the development of an "awareness" of our responsibility and power of choice to choose "not to hurt people"? When do you learn to live your life through fear and not love? Is a person conscious that they are inflicting misery, hurt and abuse on another person, and is the receiver of this pain and misery consciously or unconsciously aware that they are accepting it?

Once you are "awakened" on your spiritual journey you will be shocked to realise much of your suffering has been conditioned or learned behaviour, and it is a disconnection from your true self.

M. Scott Peck in "A Road less Travelled" said, "*The development of consciousness is the development of awareness in our conscious mind of knowledge along with our unconscious mind, which already possesses that knowledge. It is the process of the conscious mind coming into synchrony with the unconscious. Making the unconscious conscious".*

While people are unconsciously choosing chaos, cruelty, pain and suffering, if you awaken you will see your consciousness, which is "Divine Love", was you all the time but you were not aware, you were unconscious, you were existing, coping, but if you had been looking inwards, everything you needed in life was already there. We have been conditioned to look outwards rather than look inwards.

M. Scott Peck also said *"If you want to know the closest place to look for grace, it is within yourself. If you desire wisdom greater than your own, you can find it inside you. What this suggests is that the interface between God and man is at least in part the interface between our unconscious and our conscious. Our unconscious is God, within us."*

We were part of the Divine Love all the time, but where did society begin to get so disconnected? Most of us have been conditioned to "conditional love". The only problem is we have been conditioned to have a disconnection from self-value, therefore we have no self-belief and we suffer a detachment from spirit. Most people, if they looked inwards, first of all don't know what to look for, or don't know how, while the others will look inwards and self-hate.. The two most powerful emotions are love and fear. Yet modern society, with all its development and wealth, is addicted to fear. Everything is fear-based. Society is entangled with chaos, fear and hardship.

"In recovery, we learn that love is not simply a feeling. Love is an energy that is manifested by a commitment and a will to extend oneself for the purpose of nurturing one's own or another's total growth, which includes physical, mental, emotional and spiritual dimensions."

–M. SCOTT PECK, 1978

Being a co-bully, you hand over your power, your "self", to a bully who controls and manipulates you for their benefit only. A bully will certainly hurt and diminish a co-bully in any and every way possible. They will stop your self-connection, self-nurturing and will try everything to stop your self-growth.

A co-bully must break free from the pattern of putting themselves under this abusive control and change. When a co-bully lets go and connects to their "self" they will feel a peace and will no longer be addicted or co-dependent to chaos, abuse and turmoil. Love is all healing. They can feel at peace and are no longer in constant fear. A co-bully will become detached, and will witness abusive bullies but will no longer seek their approval or want to put themselves in danger. They are now an observer but are not attached to their abuse. Their journey will become effortless, fearless and limitless. A co-bully will become aware of the meaning and purpose of this spiritual journey. When you are out of self-love, you are open to abuse and in constant turmoil. Separation of self, suffering and abuse are in the place of love. So when you embrace self-love there will be no space for abuse and suffering. You must find your own holding, your home. It is being conscious of your true self, of your divine love, in union with Divine Love. It is the consciousness of embracing self-expression.

"It is the intimacy of belonging."

–JOHN O'DONOGHUE

True Self and Shadow/Ego

When we were hurt at a very young age, psychologists say from the age of three we begin to form a shadow to cope with what life threw at us. Fear is a positive message that there is a threat. Life is full of threats. But where fear overtakes our lives and we respond to everything in fear, see everything as a threat, then the shadow will overtake the true "self" and will become disconnected from the "soul". There were conditions to being loved so we got disconnected from our true "self". There were conditions to be met to be accepted, to be included, to be wanted, your presence had to be approved by other people. Fear was instilled instead of love, and out of fear grows negative emotions such as anger, jealousy and hatred. The ego thrives on fear, knowing we will have to feed our ego on fear and distract ourselves from our true path of knowing our true selves.

> *"Children cannot grow to psychological maturity in an atmosphere of unpredictability, haunted by the specter of abandonment. All children have neuroses, in that they will instinctively assume responsibility for certain deprivations that they experience but do not yet understand. Thus the child who is not loved by their parents will always assume themselves to be unlovable, rather than see the parents as deficient in their capacity to love."*

> –M SCOTT PECK

Dr Tony Humphreys in "Negative Thinking" says: "*Children start out with openness and reach out to the world in full confidence that they will be loved, cherished and nurtured. It is when this innate trust is broken, neglect, conditionality, hurt and rejection begin to occur, that children in their vast wisdom begin to evolve a means of eliminating, or at least reducing further painful experience*".

This formation of the "shadow self" is a means of coping, existing in the real world. Unfortunately, most of us become so engrossed in coping, surviving that we detach from our "true self", our connection to higher love and self-love and begin a journey wherein we respond to fear, hurt and rejection, becoming a bully or a co-bully, chaotic and false and missing out on a peaceful, joyful life. We live a life in shadow, not light. Then there are those who have totally disconnected from the true "self" and are living their ego "self", which is based on fear and over-acting, slaves to the over-demanding "world" which is totally false.

The ego is "not having the ability to show love or care". The Buddha described it as a time when *"the inability/loss goes down through the generations until someone awakens and gets in touch with their real self "love" and has the wisdom and knowledge to pass it down to their children, unconditional love."*

It takes a long time, a long journey, of self-love, self-examination and self-recovery to actually feel like you have reached a safe place, having been abused by abusers. There is a lot of self-doubt, fear of it happening again, unbelievable anxiousness about how you could have let this happen to you. How could people have done that to you? You are between two worlds and you really don't belong to either. You recognise you are a co-bully, and that you didn't have the skills to self-manage safely around another person's anger and manipulation. You are free and out of that situation but it still doesn't feel right. You don't feel right. You may become angry, which you haven't been able to do before. All this happened, your life has been damaged, you have many hurts and many losses. The abusers are still walking around the same as they did before the attacks. It is surreal, how can that be. A co-bully may feel like an outsider. A co-bully may have pain that they cannot stop. Why can't I stop feeling like this? A co-bully wants to be happy, but the pain inside feels like it is suffocating them. A co-bully will have tried to interact well, and never wanted to harm anybody. The co-bully has been brought into abusive situations over and over again, and didn't have the ability to remove him/herself from it.

A co-bully wasn't aware of self-love as a child so as an adult tries to achieve self-love with things and people outside of themselves, such as an addictions or a need for approval from other people. This internal battle with oneself, beating oneself up, being so hard on oneself, allowing other people to be so hard on you means a co-bully finds it difficult to self-love even on their road to recovery and self awareness. It takes time. Even after therapy and a long road to recovery, a co-bully may re-experience an abuser, even with awareness it may still be difficult to manage him/herself. It is very difficult for a co-bully to *toughen up*. A co-bully tries hard to understand what happened? There is self-doubt. A co-bully may find it difficult to try and start all over again, to partake and trust in company. A co-bully just wants peace. A co-bully may feel useless and now is aware that they have over and over again allowed people to bully them, all because they did not have the skills to self-manage safely. A co-bully may feel exhausted and may find it difficult to go back and engage any of the old, good feelings they used to have. A co-bully may have continuous thoughts of shame in her/his head; why didn't I do this, why didn't I do that? A co-bully may find it hard to break away from self-shaming and other people making the co-bully ashamed because they couldn't cope with abusers. It is difficult to break free of being a co-bully, but with a good support-ive network, a network that understands, it is possible to free yourself from the pattern of abusive relationships and it is possible to self-love and self-care.

J. Keith Miller says *"that at the very foundation of human experience there rages a silent hidden battle for self-esteem, for the unique identity and soul of each individual"*.

There are two sides to you, the side that appears the best you can be and the you inside who is full of self-doubt, controlling and feeling everything you do is wrong, so you end up not trusting your instincts, becoming hyper vigilant, and not **being free to just be**. Inner pain is a calling out from our souls that something is not right in our lives. Some people try to ease the pain with alcohol and drugs. Pain can be unbearable, and especially if we don't understand the source of the pain. We really have to listen deeply and hold that pain, the pain of not being perfect and not being all things to everybody.

Control

J Keith Miller says, "the feelings most relevant to control are shame and guilt".

A co-bully may feel inadequate or that they've made mistakes or feel their life is out of control. They have tried to do things right in life but they unconsciously couldn't self-manage anger and manipulation! They got entangled in situations they didn't have the exit skills to leave. They have incurred losses and hurt, and now feel shame. Shame is about feeling bad for being a person who isn't perfect, who gets things wrong instead of right. Shame seeps into every pore of their body, like a toxic chemical, which leaves them with feelings of self-doubt and feelings of no self-love or self-worth. The fear of being inadequate was projected onto children by their primary caregivers. The fear of not being good enough, smart enough, nice enough, this was absorbed by children, and they were terrified of not being good enough, not being worthy of being loved, instilling a significant fear of not being wanted and the fear of being rejected. *J. Keith Miller in COMPELLED TO CONTROL says "if we are not in touch with our feelings, then our feelings have become exaggerated, out of control. We have the volume turned off on the signal system from our unconscious". The only way to get control is to give up controlling. By living a very fast-paced life, life becomes uncontrollable and leaves us with lives that are unmanageable.*

One must find the awareness to move away from self-separation and connect to self-intimacy. A person must self-examine their journey, how and where they were conditioned to be either a co-bully or a bully. They became removed from their "real self" so they are depending on their "false self". If our prime caregivers or society has instilled in us plenty of negativity and little or no self-love, we are depending on a misinformed inner voice or advisor to help us get through the day. Our inner "true self" wants unconditional love and peace, but our "shadow self", our coping self, has been programmed for fear, for conditional love and use unhealthy strategies to survive.

The shaming voice is constantly making a person feel ashamed, inadequate, bad and not good enough. A bully will project their shame and anger and the co-bully will absorb it. Bullies are experts at projecting shaming tactics to create unease, self-doubt and disharmony in a co-bully. A co-bully usually seeks approval from others, who, are going to use it as an opportunity to diminish them or put them down. A co-bully must learn and know that they must only seek self-approval. I will mention here those powerful words, from Dr Niall Hickey, Psychotherapist and Poetry Therapist, "**I can think highly of myself irrespective of other people's opinions**". I believe these words are the start of the road to freedom for a co-bully.

God's Consciousness

Divine Love is with you every waking hour of your physical life, He is there to love you and be with you at all times, even times when your "self" has been severely tested. See it as a very loving mother or father, who only wants the best for you and will love you no matter what. Life can be full of tribulations, but with Divine Love as our loving parent we are not alone in our times of hurt and pain. You will see life as a blessing and you will see your soul as the loving part of you, not something that we could never get a grasp of. Remember you are never alone, believe and live your life through the love of life, peace and joy, even when you are severely rejected.

Higher consciousness is the consciousness of your higher-self in union with Higher Divine Love. Our "being", being consciousness is the consciousness that God is. There is no separation, only you are at one with the Divine. You are Love in union with the love of the Divine Love.

Just as we have learned on our journey that we must be conscious of our being, of our existence, of our behaviour, we must realise God's consciousness. The important thing is to seek a level of consciousness that we need to be aware of our own "self" as well as being aware of the Divine Power. If we have self-awareness then we are on the path of goodness, righteousness and we will live our lives through our own conscious being, as well as being in harmony with God's consciousness. It will be a path of love and peace. It is possible to have the presence of Love, when you have attained consciousness of your own presence in this universe. You are a spiritual being on a physical journey, to seek more awareness and live the word of Love.

Healing is that part of your journey that will transcend and take you to the "real", conscious universe. You will make the transition from a lower physical level to a higher level of healing and a loving energy. You will spiritually awaken, the old will become unfamiliar and you won't be able to relate to it in the same way. But a new world will be revealed and you will be able to express your true self, which is your inner voice, your true spirit guiding and loving you. You become you, your true nature. **It is your soul becoming visible and finding a place of expression.** Your true calling will unfold your connection and you will realize that you are here to help others. One must accept and embrace whatever happens in your life, the hurt and the joy, it is all a lesson to awaken you to the deeper mystery of your spiritual and mystical being.

You become your own artist where your true creativity, freely will flow with Divine Love onto your New Path of Life.

CHAPTER 13

To know yourself is to love your self
I am completely loved. I am
completely lovable.

Emotional Awareness

EA is the awareness of your own emotional health and how you safely interact with other people. It is the emotional health of the communicator. It is how you communicate, act, interact and react without causing distress to yourself or to another person. It is how you react to other communicators, it means you are able to self-care around aggressive and manipulative behavior without getting distressed or entangled in it. It is having a healthy self-relationship and a healthy relationship with others. It is having self-love and not permitting another person to mistreat you.

Healthy EA is being aware of your emotions, and the ability to handle life without excessive fear. You don't over react, you are calm and take time to understand the situation. You are aware of human behaviour that contributes to positive and negative feelings. You don't respond or react to unhealthy behavior.

119

A Passive EA, may be sensitive to other people's feelings and react, respond without boundaries. You may feel overwhelmed and get entangled in drama. You may get caught up reacting to other people's chaos all the time. You get over one abusive relationship until it becomes a pattern of accepting abusive behaviour; you may feel bad in relationships far more often than you *feel good*. It is not having the detached or the "observer skill".

Aggressive EA, will manipulate or respond in anger, jealousy and rage, covertly or overtly. There is total disrespect for the rights of another to have a contrary view and this person will stop at nothing to dominate, oppress and control another human being. An aggressive EA has no boundaries, is devious, ruthless and has no empathy.

Emotional Intelligence, as a psychological theory, was developed by *Peter Salovey* and *John Mayer*.

> *"Emotional intelligence is the ability to perceive emotions, to access and generate emotions so as to assist thought, to understand emotions and emotional knowledge, and to reflectively regulate emotions so as to promote emotional and intellectual growth."*
>
> —MAYER & SALOVEY, 1997

Self-awareness

Is the ability to understand your pattern of behavior in relationships and how you emotionally respond to other people's pattern of behaviour. It is being free from co-dependency and attachment. It is how you see yourself, if you have self-love and self-care or if you have self-doubt, self-hate or self-harm. It is how you interact with another person, e.g. do you have chronic approval dependency or have the need for acceptance and inclusion? Do you look outward or look inwards to feel good. It is how you feel about yourself. It is understanding your history, recoding your memory and stopping the self-sabotage of your happiness. It is liberation and empowerment. It is the awareness of your own emotional state and how you react to another's emotional state. You cannot interact with EA until you know your own EA. It is the awareness of another's unhealthy emotional state and not taking it personally. **When we don't know our own feelings, we are left to rely on others and their empathy or lack of empathy. On those who haven't self-examined so their responses are unpredictable.** It is awareness of relationship skills that are healthy and those that are not healthy. Identify whether you communicate passively or aggressively. A person must heal and understand the root of how they learned their unhealthy communication patterns and how their emotional health was affected by it. With awareness it is possible to change and embrace healthy communication skills. Know the triggers that disempower you.

Observer Self

Is the ability to see a situation or relationship for what it is. When you are attached in relationships, you are locked in a conditioned role with little understanding of what is actually happening. There may be a lot of suffering, but if you detach with awareness and witness your own behavior and the other's behavior towards you, you can see it as healthy or unhealthy and self-manage safely in both. Create your observer self.

Thoughts

Think calm and positive thoughts. Develop the ability to recognize when another person is "dumping" their negative thoughts on you. Develop the ability to recognise negative thoughts and release them without causing internal hurt and long-term pain. Develop the ability to change your pattern of negative thinking. Remove yourself from lower consciousness to higher consciousness. Have awareness of the emotional state of other people before you interact with them on a personal level. Do not judge other people, and do not accept their negative judgment as normal and think before you interact. Embrace people's differences and be open to change.

Relationships

To have healthy communication skills which lead to loving and supportive relationships. We must be proactive and not react to others letting the world dictate to us. We must reach our optimum self-growth and take the responsibility to create our own world. We can change our acceptance of absorbing other people's negative thoughts and our own personal negative thoughts, perceptions and interpretations embedded in our psyche. We must not accept other people's negative thoughts and actions that affect our well-being. We can begin to enjoy life and the people we choose to invite into our life on a daily basis.

Spirituality

The freedom to self-love, to know you are part of a higher love. To see goodness, contribute to the wellness of the world, to be positive and grateful. To treat everyone well and know everyone is on their physical journey and support them, rather than making their journey painful. To have empathy and understand some people are carrying deep emotional pain. To understand unexamined people will disconnect you from your core or spiritual self. You must reconnect to your core, your spiritual self and connect to Divine Love.

Listening Skills

Most people listen to reply not to understand.

When we are communicating with another person we assume that they understand what we are trying to communicate. When a bully is communicating it is "TUNNEL LISTENING", they listen without understanding or having empathy. A co-bully believes that their message has been understood empathically. A co-bully needs to be aware and understand, that it is only necessary to respond to what you want to respond to *not* to what you feel you are forced to respond to. A co-bully must have **power over their own response** and just be aware a bully may be listening only to attack or create conflict and use what you are saying rather than listening with empathy or understanding.

Communication Skills

Assertive – Healthy communication skills

Passive – Submissive, Receptive of unhealthy communication

Direct – Aggression, (covert/overt)

Indirect – Manipulation, deceit, betrayal

Moving Forward with Skills to Manage Your Emotional Safety

To move forward and have the skills to self-manage around aggression and manipulation a person needs to take the following steps.

1. Awareness you are a co-bully and at this point you may not be in a safe place, but get to a safe place

2. Love, Care and Protect yourself and EXPRESS your personal boundary and do not permit anybody to disrespect your space. Respect those who respect you

3. Get a HEALTHY SUPPORT network and surround yourself in safety. Ask for support, you are not alone

4. Become self-aware and begin your journey of self-examination and self-wisdom

5. Detach and assert your separateness from the aggressor or manipulator

6. Detach and know their negative behaviour is nothing to do with you

7. Emerge your observer self, with clearer awareness you can observe more safely and with this knowledge, understand your role, the healthy or unhealthy interaction between people

8. Start your journey of self-love, self-care and self-forgiveness

9. Seek therapy and get to the root of where you began to accept unsafe behavior

10. Self-forgiveness for not having the skills to self-manage up to now

11. Recover from co-dependency

12. Let go of the pain. Acknowledge the pain, and with time heal it and release it

13. No longer accept aggressive, manipulative behaviour as NORMAL

14. Embrace spirituality

15. Change from being an acceptor or passive communicator to being an ASSERTIVE communicator

16. Look inwards for approval, not outwards

17. Take time, before you get involved with anybody emotionally

18. Know your boundaries, create boundaries and protect your boundaries

19. Know there is only one of you, you are uniquely special, and you are SEPARATE, love you and your differences

20. Connect to your "love" within, know that is all you need and live your life through love, not fear

Self-Love V Materiality Love

Self-fulfillment is arriving at a place where you self-love and self-forgive. It is awareness of your love within and you can be your "self". It is self-actualisation or self–realisation. It is being consciously connected to "self" and connected to a Higher consciousness. It is being connected to your inner love which is connected to Higher love. It is being at peace within. A place where you recognize your journey, understand it, accept it, embrace it and be grateful for all your past, present and future. You are where you are meant to be. It is inner self-fulfillment, of knowing yourself, looking inward and feeling loveable, rather than looking outward for acceptance or material wealth. The most important wealth on this journey is the gift or treasure of inner love, and having inner peace. When we have personal fulfillment it is only then that we can be in a place to enjoy material fulfillment. When you are joyful within it is then that you can experience real outer joy and fulfillment. When we have inner love, inner forgiveness it is then that we can extend and relate to others through love, understanding and forgiveness.

Meditation

Bless this space between us.

–JOHN O'DONOGHUE

Meditation is how you begin to understand, connect and be aware of your "self". Meditation gives you the time, silence and the space to reflect on your inner spiritual and emotional state. You take time with your "self", you connect to your soul, your love within and extend your love to Higher Love and the Universe. It is a state of bliss and gratefulness. This is the time to connect to your positive energy which in turn connects to the universe's positive energies. How you experience the world, the situations that you attract, and the situations you are attracted to, are extensions or mirrors of your inner spiritual and emotional state. Your inner emotional state is reflected out on your outer emotional state. Before this you were in chaos, emotionally disconnected, emotionally unavailable, it was also what you were attracted to and what was attracted to you. Now following recovery and self-connection you can begin to connect and attract more peaceful, joyful and a self-fulfilling life. We connect to our hearts, our spirit and what feels true and right for us. We release and disconnect to all negative energies. We connect to the power within, our self-power with the will, the intention to create a life that we want. Our emotions are healed and flowing, which it is purest energy connection to our true-self which in turn is connected to Higher Love and Power. We become self-empowered and we can aspire to be, to emerge our true "self", our true "nature".

A dancing breeze touches my face
I feel I'm in a state of grace…
Come, hold my hand and walk with me
Paradise on earth is being free…

Thoughts

You are a Soul

You're soul wants to be your "self"
I never took time to know my "self"
To know yourself is to love your "self"
I am completely loved. I am completely lovable.

–JC

Support –Support –Support

Support – taking you by a kind hand out of the darkness.

–JC

There is a centre in the body where love and spirit are joined, and that centre is the heart

Nobody has a Right to Judge you

Or put you down, if you understand that, and ignore all those
unfounded and unwarranted "put downs", and know the only
One you have to answer to is Divine Love, who has made you in
his image which is pure and goodness. You must learn to cherish
yourself and never let another's unconscious behaviour upset or
disconnect you. When you become self-aware you will realize all
those negative remarks about you, DO NOT, actually reflect who
you are. We become upset with these diminishing remarks, but you
will see when you are detached, it is their own mismanaged feelings
they are projecting. Who are they to judge you?

–JC

Awareness

I am standing on the same beautiful spot overlooking the sea,
yesterday I was in Hell, today I am in Heaven
the difference: *I have removed myself from the path of negativity*
I now choose to surround myself with peaceful people.

–JC

Discipline

Disciplinary traumas (corporal punishment/hitting/physical
abuse) are encoded in the brain, stunting our ability to overcome
them. Our bodies retain memories of humiliation, causing
a panoply of physical ills and dangerous levels of denial.

–ALICE MILLER

Emotional Abusers abuse because they can, through an accepted
negative behaviour pattern. Nobody has confronted them, to make
them "aware" that their abusive behaviour is not acceptable, or
they just don't listen *when they are asked to stop hurting people.*
First recognise it is abuse, then say a big "STOP" and get out.

–JC

The co-bully is at an immediate disadvantage when it comes to
confrontation. The bully can verbally defend him/herself, because
they express; the co-bully suppresses, often believing they don't
have a place or the right to be heard.

–JC

The formation of the fragile, pleaser, to a lifetime of acceptance
of negative emotional targeting, rejection and abandonment.
The fragile, frightened, Child within stays too long in an
abusive situation.

–JC

I listen to your opinion, but I also have an opinion even if it is
different from yours.

–JC

Whether a co-bully is a deliberate target or an innocent bystander, the emotionally abused child will struggle deeply to "explain" the conduct of his/her abusers—and ends up struggling for survival in a turmoil of self-blame and self-doubt.

Stop playing the role of the Pleaser, it only gets you entangled
with people who will see it as an opportunity to use, deceive and
emotionally abuse you. I'm free to please me even when it
may not please you.

–JC

Your struggle matters because I care about you, but it does not
control how I feel about myself.

Detach yourself from negative, harmful people. Stop trying to
please people, stop being available. The bully's main weapon is
to project guilt and shame. While the bully is dismantling your life
bit by bit, they are feathering their own nest, your loss is their gain.

Remember you have done nothing wrong, and stop self-blaming.
Before you trust a person, take time to know them and only trust
them when they interact healthily. Because the bully is often
someone you have connected with, whom you trusted,
the hurt can go very deep. The only person you can change
is yourself, you will never change a bully – stop trying!

-JC

I felt I wanted to burst out of prison, only to realise they were
psychological barriers, and the door was open all the time!

-JC

I didn't know that I had a right to keep my "self"
safe and protect myself.

-JC

Treat me as I want to be treated – with Respect and Dignity.

-JC

Crest of a wave, Whirl of the wind, Flame of a fire,
"I" must emerge and just be Love is Spirit, Spirit is the Self.

-JC

No one person is responsible for your disconnection
it is universal disconnection and unawareness.

-JC

Abusers are soul snatchers because they violate and disconnect your soul and leave you with a grave sense of no "self". They coerce you into a state of loss and a state of fear all the time while you struggle to claw out and escape the abuse that is being forced on you.

–JC

An Emotional Crisis – An Emotional Cripple,

When it is time, when you are in CRYSIS, when you need to find your safe Place of Belonging, you can only emerge safely with conscious people who are in their own Place of Belonging.

–JC

I am a supreme spiritual being, the Divine loves me for being me.

–MARY KING

God is so magnificent that at best, man has made but a futile attempt to convey his greatness.

–MARY KING

A bully will argue all the time, just for argument's sake.

–JC

Hurt people, hurt people.

Some people that help the most may get hurt the most.

–JIMMY BROWNE, MIACP

Attachment is suffering, detach, assert separateness and witness their behaviour. You are empowering yourself.

> *Life is self-creative. Use your life to create your "self" as who you*
> *are, and who you've always wanted to be.*
>
> —NEALE DONALD WALSCH

It is not about changing your "self", it is about finding your "self".

Break free from the role that was imposed on you. A co-bully has a very high approval dependency. Remove your "self" from negative, argumentative circles, be peaceful and free outside the emotionally abusive cycle.

> *I exist as I am.*
>
> —WALT WHITMAN

> *How can you find love in someone's heart when it is not there?*
> *How can you expect love from someone when there is only*
> *bitterness and anger.*
>
> —MIGUEL RUIZ

The one who surrenders the need to control, wins the struggle of trying to control, Life cannot be controlled.

> *It appears the co-bully is getting on fine in an emotional abusive*
> *environment, **but** is struggling greatly to express freely and safely.*
>
> —JC

You do not deserve to be abused,
it can STOP with the right help and support.

–JC

Pain results from a judgment you have made about a thing.
Remove the judgment and the pain disappears.

–Neale Donald Walsch

The obstacle of an unconscious sense of guilt...
as the most powerful of all obstacles to recovery.

–Freud

The world is a dangerous place to live;
not because of the people who are evil,
but because of the people who don't do anything about it.

–Albert Einstein

The love that you are outwardly searching for, is the love that is closest to you, WITHIN.

The feeling of pain is our friend trying to save us,
to lead us out of danger into recovery.

–J.Keith Miller

I looked in the mirror and saw my reflection,
I looked inside my "self" and saw me.

-JC

Suffering may make us question life and lead us to the path of peace, sometimes people have to truly suffer for the hero or heroine to emerge.

When love and spirit are brought together, their power can
accomplish anything, then love, power, and spirit are one.

–DEEPAK CHOPRA

Emotional abuse: the scars are not physically visible,
but you are walking on egg shells every day
unarmed in hostile captivity.

-JC

I am powerless, I have given my power to you.

-JC

Let your fragile self be supported and cared for by Divine Love.

You know that you have fully experienced love
when you turn into love – that is the spiritual goal of life.

–DEEPAK CHOPRA

*Peace is the result of retraining your mind **to process life as it is**, rather than as you think it should be.*

–DR WAYNE DYER

Go with the flow of life. There are always going to be challenges but it is how you deal with them. Self-love and self-belief will keep you balanced and know that life keeps changing so embrace life's experiences they are temporary.

What part of "no" or "stop" don't you understand? Set the RULES and your boundaries between anyone you communicate with.

We must begin to look at the bigger picture, realise and understand that this neglect and abuse is not only in our "space" but has gone down through time and generations. We must self-awake and create awareness that all of us can choose a life of love in connection with the love of the Universe and stop abuse going down from one generation to the next.

Look inwards to understand other people's negative behavior towards you, be aware their behavior is nothing to do with you, **you did not cause their behavior**, you don't have to discuss or criticize them, just be aware they are not consciously aware of their "negative behaviour", assert your separateness, self-protect and self-love in their company.

You are enough, self-accept and self-love.
You have a right to do what is best for you.
You need to be aware, that not everybody you meet is "good" for you.
You'll know you're on the right road when you stop looking back…

References

Codependent No More	Melody Beattie
The Language of Letting Go	Melody Beattie
Healing the Child Within	Charles. L. Whitfield M.D.
Your Sacred Self	Dr. Wayne W. Dyer
The Path to Love	Deepak Chopra
Conversations with God	Neale Donald Walsch
Who's Life are you Living?	Tony Humphreys
Self-Esteem: The Key to Your Child's Education	Tony Humphreys
Compelled to Control	J. Keith Miller
The Mastery of Love	Don Miguel Ruiz
Starting Over: Learning to Love Yourself	Linda Ellis Eastman
The Road Less Travelled	M. Scott Peck
Anam Cara	John O'Donohue
Readings for Recovery	C B Keogh D. D., Ph.D
How to Get What You Want, And Want What You Have	John Gray